Double Tongue

by

Brian Woolland

This edition of *Double Tongue* published in 2003 by:
Border Crossings Ltd.
13, Laburnum Close,
Poplar Grove
LONDON
N11 3NR

Tel / Fax: +44 (0) 20 8361 2308
email: books@bordercrossings.org.uk
website: www.bordercrossings.org.uk

Border Crossings Registered Charity No. 1048836

A catalogue record for this book is available from the British Library.

ISBN 1-904718-01-9

Printed by Marva Printers

Introduction to *Double Tongue*
by Teresa Murjas

"Now cometh the sin of double-tongue, such as speak fair before folk and wickedly behind."
(Geoffrey Chaucer, Canterbury Tales)

"We watch CNN. Practically everyone can see CNN at all times - CNN, Sky, BBC. It can all be seen here. Nothing special. They are paid to lie."
(Slobodan Milošević, CBS Interview)

"We are putting both our air space and our airports at NATO's disposal, but that does not mean participation in military action."
(Janos Martyni, Hungarian Foreign Minister, Magyar Nemzet Inteview)

It is Spring 1999. Important political developments take place in the Balkans. On March 12th Hungary joins NATO. Ministers in Budapest - the capital city and one of the settings for *Double Tongue* - assert that NATO accession will finally put an end to the Yalta world order. The Hungarian nation can set about creating an atmosphere of security. Membership of NATO will help the government act effectively in the face of cross-frontier threats, such as organised crime, drug trafficking and illegal migration.

However, Hungary now enjoys the unenviable distinction of being the only NATO member to share a southern border of over 170 km with Serbia. There, almost twelve years ago, Slobodan Milošević transformed himself into a firebrand of Serbian nationalism, helping to prize the lid off ethnic and nationalistic rivalries and set Yugoslavia on a course of fragmentation, conflict and violence. The complex federal structures of the country have been gradually dismembered by wars that have successively pitted Serbs and Serbia against Slovenes, Croats and Bosnian Muslims. Tactics of ethic cleansing now proliferate. Streams of refugees are a common phenomenon. Bill Clinton has described the Balkans as 'a tinderbox'.

It is Spring 1999. Conflict rages in Kosovo, Serbia's southernmost province and Yugoslavia's dominant republic. Kosovo has, in the past, often been pointed to as a centre of the Western Multicultural idea. With the rise of nationalist rhetoric in the Balkans, mono-ethnic notions of Croats, Bosnians and Serbs have been highlighted. Many Serbs regard Kosovo as the cradle of their nation and the birthplace of Serbian orthodox religion. Albanians - in the main Moslem - comprise 90% of its population and many argue that they are the descendants of its original inhabitants. The result - war in Kosovo. Atrocities perpetrated by the Yugoslav military - including executions and mass deportations of the Albanian civilian population. Milošević refuses to sign the Rambouillet peace accord.

Roughly two weeks after Hungarian accession, NATO launches its bombing campaign on Kosovo. There is no traditional military objective - the stated aims are to stop the slaughter on humanitarian grounds and to prevent the war from spreading. Initially, the air strikes are focused on weakening Yugoslav air defences. This progresses towards the destruction of equipment used by their ground forces. The ethnic Albanian 'guerrillas' of the KLA call for NATO to send in ground forces in order to protect Albanians and expel the Serbs.

The Hungarian Republic has answered affirmatively to a request by NATO to allow military aircraft to fly through its airspace and to take off and land on its territory. Debate rages. Hungary's role in the war is to be one of 'passive support' for intervention. But speculation is rife that NATO may attempt to involve the country in a more complex way by launching a ground attack from its territory.

There is another issue. Hungary is the only NATO member with an ethnic minority of roughly 300,000 living in the Northern Yugoslav province of Vojvodina. Will offering too much support for NATO's action spark a Serb backlash against these people? The Vojvodina is a multi-lingual environment. School pupils are taught in Serbian, but Hungarian has for many years been referred to officially as 'the language of the social surroundings.' Will these people be regarded as 'Yugoslavians' when in Hungary, and Hungarian when in 'Yugoslavia'?

To cap it all, global concern about the US role in world affairs has been rising for some time. NATO has been denounced for resorting to Imperialist methods of warfare, particularly since UN authorisation to proceed with the bombardment of a sovereign state has not been given. Perhaps air power will not put a *stop* to ethnic cleansing, but *intensify* it. Instances of civilian casualties of the bombing have significantly damaged the credibility of NATO's aims. In Russia, the Serbs are perceived as Slavic Davids under attack by an American Goliath. In Moscow, images of President Clinton are torched, the US Embassy is pelted with eggs, ink and beer bottles.

It is April 1999. Szeged - Hungary's third largest city and the other setting for Woolland's play - swarms with foreign and local journalists, and cameramen. They are seeking out a safe, NATO guaranteed, base from which to venture into Yugoslavia. Some set up their equipment on the rooftops. Hotel reservations are up from 50 to 70%. It is perhaps true to say that - in multiple ways - money will flow from a place where shots are fired. At times of instability, trade of all kinds will inevitably be conducted.

These are the historical and political events with which *Double Tongue* 'converses'. The play's dominant themes and dilemmas emerge directly from a fascinated preoccupation with real and startlingly relevant issues, particularly given subsequent global events. It explores a set of developing relationships between five characters and a religious icon. It demonstrates how the confrontation and mutual interpretation of these six constructed identities - of six sets of experiences, desires and partially concealed motivations - create an explosion of aggression driven largely by different kinds of desperation. This explosion reflects the tension, brutality and confusion of a wider conflict with deep historical roots, a conflict played out in 1999; but one that will always, it seems, remain contemporary. Border Crossings' two productions of *Double Tongue* took place on either side of September 11th 2001. In its October 2002 revival, the play had inevitably acquired added urgency and immediacy for a Western audience.

Differing and juxtaposed perspectives are important in this compassionate and politically astute play. Possibilities for their development are presented in the fact that this text forms the basis for a multi-media performance, with voices and images on tape interacting with onstage action to form a carefully constructed visual and aural polyphony. The ending arises from the aggressive accumulation of all these perspectives, and was, in this production, worthy of a Revenge Tragedy. The audience are confronted with two dead bodies (an American and a Serb), two wounded men (one British, one a black Hungarian) and a woman holding a gun (Hungarian, of Jewish extraction). The location is her flat in Szeged. Those who have killed are not necessarily those whom we would have expected to become killers. The fact remains that the woman has, to varying degrees, sanctioned these men's incursions onto her territory. Ultimately, however, she finds that she must intervene.

Woolland titles each of his scenes a 'unit'. The structure of the play parodies and exploits that of a Hungarian language tape and puts the audience 'in role' as pupils. The Border Crossings production took place in three languages - English, Hungarian and Serbo-Croat. Unless you can understand all three (less likely in the UK, no doubt, than 'Eastern Europe') there will always be times when behavioural clues given by actors are sought in order to help re-construct meaning. Thus the multiple functions of language in a variety of encounters- communication, concealment, arousal, provocation - are thrown into sharp relief, and notions of translation, mediation and interpretation problematised.

When on tour in Debrecen and Budapest, the company have noted vocal audience identification with the complex political and emotional nuances of Anna's unfortunate predicament. This also occurs when Hungarian speakers comprise a significant proportion of UK audiences - a frequent, and celebrated, occurrence. The director, Michael Walling, comments that this apparent identification - a choice of perspective, perhaps - is signalled most overtly through laughter. It is to be remarked that different 'cultural contingencies' within an audience often express an amused reaction at significantly different moments of the performance. This can perhaps be seen as largely dependent on a few main factors. What is the extent and context of their bi (or tri) -lingualism? Do they have a strong sense of being part of a specific group? Do they consciously (or unconsciously) instigate a process of 'cultural positioning' in relation to evolving perceptions about other audience members? What is their relationship with - and attitude towards - the various political standpoints expressed in the play? In Szeged itself, different audience members understood all three languages to varying degrees. This led to a particularly dynamic performance in which linguistic and political tensions in the auditorium were expressed on stage, and vice versa.

In a Western context, many audience members will probably find themselves relating to (though not necessarily empathising with) Robert, an American PhD student who arrives in Eastern Europe in order to conduct research into religion after the Changes. What is the exact extent of Robert's naivety? He appears to assume that the Changes are over. He thinks that his position as researcher will guarantee him neutrality in any conflict. He begins by treating the topic of his research, though highly problematic to his subjects, as rather abstract, associated with buildings rather than individuals and relationships. This is perhaps inevitable given that he cannot speak a single East European language. Perhaps he assumes that he doesn't need to. After all, he has his Rough Guide with him.

Luckily, he finds himself a translator. They begin an affair. Their mutual attraction is complicated by a number of factors. Anna is involved with three other men. One of them is James, a British 'art dealer' who uses her language school as a respectable front for money laundering activities and a neat trade in religious icons. Another is Milan, a well-travelled and educated Serb whose plan for stopping the conflict in Kosovo involves a rifle of British manufacture. Finally, there is her reportedly ageing and increasingly senile father, a survivor of the Belsen concentration camp, whom we never see. He is arguably someone who might benefit from the apparent comforts of an American lifestyle.

James exploits his status and income as a Western dealer in cultural goods to pay for sex with B, an androgynous black prostitute and the epitome, from his perspective, of the desirable exotic artefact. So desirable, in fact, that he attempts to strike a clean deal to purchase B from a pimp whom he automatically assumes to have connections with the Russian mafia. When B arrives battered and bruised at Anna's apartment in Szeged, things come to a head.

A cacophony of disputation is created. Having humiliated Robert sexually, Milan becomes fanatically determined to regard him as an imperialist coloniser, a sinister stereotype, representative of his nation. Robert is both sexually attracted to and loathes Milan. Perhaps his conscience has been pricked. Could he really be the embodiment of that most terrible, least politically correct, phenomenon - the American cultural tourist? Anna loves Milan so intensely that she fears the impact of his understandably bigoted point of view. In an attempt to assert her own sense of impotence, she makes a cruel show of humiliating B. James struggles with great finesse to maintain a stiff upper lip, but even his meticulously tailored sophistication and understated machismo begin to unravel. All these opposing tendencies contribute towards what might be seen as a breakdown in communication. If, that is, you believe violence to be a last resort.

The man who is at once the least and most dangerous - Robert - is the first to kill, though not the first to be provoked. Cornered, he strangles Milan in an absolute frenzy and Anna, revealing more about herself through aggression than she has ever done through conversation, shoots Robert. The more fragmented, ambiguous and fluid stable notions of identity become, the more do objectives and prejudices seem to crystallize into violent action. A rise in adrenaline may sharpen the faculties, but do sharpened faculties necessarily guarantee clear sight?

Woolland builds tension by gradually and enticingly revealing contradictions about his characters and by fragmenting stage action. In this production, we eventually see events taking place in separate rooms in Anna's apartment played out simultaneously. The 'language tape' is rewound in order to permit juxtapositions that facilitate different emphases. Dominated by the central image of Szeged - a city balanced precariously on the knife-edge of a border - all this serves to evoke an atmosphere of duplicity, ambiguity, indecision and uncertainty. The resultant fluidity flaws attempts at mediation and confounds all attempts at 'honest trade'.

This tendency towards fragmentation finds its anchor in the figure of the Black Madonna. As James explains, statues and icons of the Black Madonna can be found all over Europe. They are mainly of mediaeval origin, of dark or black features, frequently regarded as miraculous and venerated by members of the Catholic and Orthodox churches. Some academic studies have suggested that certain of these art forms 'turned black' as a result of particular physical factors, such as accumulated smoke from votive candles or the deterioration of lead-based pigments.

More dramatic - and possibly implausible - legends are related during the play in association with both Madonnas presented. By allowing the embodiment of the stolen/rescued Bosnian icon and giving her a voice - frequently laden with irony - Woolland arguably comes closest to unambiguously eking out his own perspective. Her overt connection with B (they are played by the same actor) creates a particular series of tensions. B is, in James' description, located on the bottom rung of the Hungarian 'social ladder' - hence, no doubt, the limited choice of profession available to him. Both B and the icon, given their blackness - their, in this context, remarked upon and politicised otherness - are subject to more aggressive and overt readings that evolve according to the racial and cultural prejudices of other characters. Thus, they recall the numerous other victims of European intolerance and genocide. Can the veneration of an icon depicting a black woman and her child ever be less problematic than communicating with - than touching - a black woman and her child? An impulse exhibited by all the characters - including B himself - to possess and exoticise the other is rationalised by means of a process of objectification, an attempt to diffuse its perceived threat. B's attempts to survive by trading his sexual favours for a dangerous form of security will undoubtedly never be regarded socially as on a par with James' trade in weapons and cultural artefacts, given the inequalities in these men's power relations, which are of course symptomatic of their social context. But from a moral perspective? Well, that is, of course, a different matter.

The symbiotic relationship between B and the Black Madonna forms, as it were, the eye of the cyclone, a centre of semantic potency around which notions of race, sexuality, gender, institutionalised religion and capitalism co-exist in a state of perpetual debate. It brilliantly draws attention to the ideologies that we develop in order to perpetuate them and which prevent us from finding peaceful solutions. Perhaps a peaceful solution is the last thing we want.

"Prisitna used to be such a nice place," she said, referring to the capital of the Serbian province of Kosovo. "Now every house and every mosque is on fire. Serbian families write 'S' on their doors. If you don't have an 'S', the Serb gangs come to burn and kill."

(Albanian Muslim refugee in Turkey, New York Times)

Teresa Murjas
2003

Teresa Murjas is a Lecturer in Theatre at Reading University. She is bilingual in Polish and English.

Double Tongue was commissioned by Border Crossings with an Arts Council of England New Writing Award. It was first presented by Border Crossings at the Old Red Lion, London, on June 19th 2001.

Cast (in order of appearance)

Anna Kovács	*Krisztina Erdélyi*
Robert Lee	*Ben Pitts*
James Hart	*Giles Foreman*
B / Black Madonna	*Christopher Simpson*
Milan	*Serge Soric*

with
Eszter Pataki as the Newsreader

Directed by	**Michael Walling**
Designed by	**Kimie Nakano**
Lighting by	**Marc Rosette**
Assistant Director	**Susan Weaver**
Stage Manager	**Sarah Pearce**
Chinook Sound by	**Jem Kelly**
Icon made by	**Nisha Walling**

The production was subsequently revived, with some revisions to the script, for a tour of Hungary and the UK. This edition incorporates the revisions. The revival opened at the Old Synagogue in Szeged on September 17th 2002. The cast and crew were the same, except that James was played by David Farnworth and B / Black Madonna by Arnie Hewitt. Fights were directed by Alison de Burgh, the Assistant Director was Rosanna Lowe, the Administrator was Christopher Corner and the Stage Manager was Paul St. John-Shaw. The 2002 tour was funded by the Arts Council of England and the Hungarian Ministry of Culture.

DOUBLE TONGUE

The play is set in April 1999 in Budapest and in Szeged, a town close to the border between Hungary and Serbia.

CHARACTERS

ROBERT LEE	an American in his late twenties. He is trying to learn to speak Hungarian.
ANNA KOVÁCS	a Hungarian woman in her mid twenties. She speaks excellent English. She has black hair and a slightly Jewish appearance.
JAMES HART	a well spoken Englishman in his late thirties. He speaks some Hungarian - but not often.
MILAN (pronounced Meelan)	a Serb in his early thirties. He also speaks Hungarian and English. He has studied at the University in Szeged and has lived for some time in America.
B....	an androgynous male prostitute, sometimes known as Belle, working from a night-club in Budapest. Played by the same actor who plays The Black Madonna.
THE BLACK MADONNA	an androgynous young woman who appears to be in her early twenties. She speaks in the dominant language of the audience - i.e. English OR Hungarian. She and B are NOT the same character, although the two roles should be played by the same actor.

NOTES ON THE TEXT

Where there are dots in the text this indicates slight pauses. The number of dots indicates the length of the pause: ..   ...   or   ....

Where *silence*   is marked, it should always be played; and should be markedly longer than a four dot pause.

Dialogue ending with a dash —   indicates that the next character interrupts.

Where the dialogue is marked with a forward slash (/), the next speaker starts at that point and the dialogue overlaps.

Occasionally a character is attributed with question mark as a 'line' of dialogue to indicate a quizzical expression. Thus:

     ROBERT   ?

In this draft of the text most of the dialogue is written in English. Where the dialogue is in italics, the character should be speaking in Hungarian; and will need translating. Some of Milan's dialogue is in Hungarian, and some in English; some of Anna's is in English, some of it in Hungarian. There are a few occasions where Milan speaks Serbo-Croat. This is indicated by italics with an (S-C) at the end of the line / speech.

ANNA's VOICE:
When the play is performed for an English audience Anna's Voice (on the language school tape) should be in Hungarian and English for the title and English for the description of the unit. For a Hungarian audience, the English version of the unit titles should be followed by the Hungarian; the description of the unit should then be in Hungarian.

THE TITLES, but not the full unit descriptions, should also appear throughout each scene as projections - in the language of the country in which the play is being performed.

———————————————————————

Szeged is pronounced Sseggedd, NOT Shegg ed. The emphasis on the first syllable. The z makes the s

sibilant, and is NOT sounded as a z would be in English.

PART ONE - Getting to know people

<u>UNIT One</u>   **The Language School.**

Anna talks directly to the audience, as if to a new class of students.

WHILE THE LANGUAGE SCHOOL PUBLICITY TAPE PLAYS, **ROBERT** IS WORKING WITH
A TAPE RECORDER ON HIS OWN DESK.

ANNA's VOICE (on the language school tape):
Jó estét. Kovács Anna vagyok. Good evening. My name is Anna Kovács. I would
like to welcome you to our language school. For some of you, I know, this is your
first visit to Budapest. So, welcome also to Hungary's beautiful and very lively
Capital City.

In our language laboratory, your teacher will occasionally listen in to your work.
She can switch between any of her students; and you can always be sure of personal
assistance when you need it.

**ANNA's VOICE (heard through loudspeakers - as ROBERT hears it on the language school tape – also
appears on surtitle apparatus):**
The first unit is called: *Jó estét.* Good evening.

ROBERT   Jó estét.

ANNA's VOICE   Kovács Anna vagyok.   My name is Anna Kovács

ROBERT   Robert Lee vagyok.   Sorry.   Lee Robert vagyok.
                       My name is Robert Lee.

ANNA's VOICE   *How are you?*

ROBERT   *I am fine.*

ANNA's VOICE   *What are you doing here in Hungary?*

HE HAS TO REPEAT THIS ONE TO UNDERSTAND THE QUESTION.

ROBERT   *I am ....*
                       Damn. Sorry. I know what I'm doing it's just that I don't know how to say it in
                       Hungarian.   *I don't know how to say it.*

ANNA'S VOICE   *You must try to speak in Hungarian.*   In Hungarian please.

ROBERT   *Yes.*

ANNA's VOICE   *What was the question?*

ROBERT   What am I doing here in Hungary.

ANNA's VOICE   In Hungarian.

ROBERT   *Yes.*

ANNA's VOICE   Repeat the question in Hungarian.

ROBERT LOOKS CAREFULLY AT HIS NOTES AND STARTS TO PREPARE WHAT
HE IS GOING TO SAY.   HE IS UNAWARE THAT **ANNA** IS NOW STANDING BEHIND
HIM.

1

ROBERT   Bloody Hell. OK. Here goes. *Lee Robert vagyok.* *I am American.* *I come from*
                          Montana, but now I live in New York. *I am in Budapest because I am working here*
                          in Hungary.

ANNA   Good. You are getting better.

ROBERT   Oh....   I thought you were... (POINTING TO THE HEADPHONES, AND
          GRINNING RATHER FOOLISHLY).

          HE IS STARTLED BY FINDING HER THERE SO CLOSE TO HIM. AND IS CAUGHT OFF
          GUARD. HE FINDS HER VERY ATTRACTIVE.

                          Hello...

ANNA   And what is your *'work'* ?

ROBERT   I'm doing some research.

ANNA   Interesting?

ROBERT   But I don't know how to talk about it in Hungarian.

ANNA   Early days.

ROBERT   It's difficult enough to explain it in English.

ANNA   Try.

          THEY LOOK AT EACH OTHER. UNCERTAIN. **ROBERT** NODS. SMILES. COLLECTS HIS
          PAPERS AND TEXT BOOK FROM THE DESK TOP, PUTS THEM IN THE BACK-PACK THAT
          ACCOMPANIES HIM EVERYWHERE. AS HE IS DOING THIS —

TAPED VOICE   Now, to finish off with, I would like you to revise what we have done today.
                          Imagine you are meeting someone for the first time. You want to tell them who you
                          are, what you are doing in Hungary, and anything else about yourself that you think
                          would be interesting.

UNIT Two   The Budapest Bar

          TWO BAR STOOLS, A LONG WAY APART. **B.** IS SITTING ON ONE, DRINKING SLOWLY.
          HIS HEAD IS TURNED AWAY, SO THAT HIS FACE IS ONLY PARTLY VISIBLE TO THE
          AUDIENCE. IT IS UNCERTAIN WHETHER HE IS MAN OR WOMAN. THERE IS
          SOMETHING FLIRTATIOUS, PROVOCATIVE ABOUT HIS POSE. HE SEEMS BOTH SELF-
          CONTAINED AND VULNERABLE. HE OCCASIONALLY TAKES A DRINK, BUT OTHERWISE
          DOES NOTHING.

          JAMES COMES IN TO THE BAR. HE CARRIES AN UMBRELLA, AN AIRMAIL COPY OF
          THE TIMES AND A CATALOGUE FROM AN AUCTION OF ART NOUVEAU SCULPTURE
          AND GLASSWARE. HE GESTURES TO A BARMAN (WHO IS NOT SEEN), AND IS GIVEN A
          WHISKY AND SODA.

          FROM THE MOMENT HE COMES IN HE IS ATTRACTED TO **B.** HE READS HIS
          CATALOGUE, MAKES SOME NOTES ON A LAP-TOP COMPUTER (CIRCA 1999!). **B.** LOOKS
          OVER TOWARDS HIM. **JAMES** GLANCES UP. THEIR LOOKS MEET.

          B. SMILES AT HIM.

2

<u>UNIT Three</u>   **The foyer of an International hotel in Szeged.**

ANNA's VOICE (on the language school tape):
> The title of this unit is *'Hová akar menni?'* Where do you want to go?
> In this unit you will learn how to make friends; how to offer somebody a drink; and how to accept or refuse an invitation.

ANNA SITTING ON A SOFA ON THE EDGE OF THE LARGE FOYER SPACE. ROBERT RETURNS FROM GETTING THEIR DRINKS. GIVES ANNA A GLASS OF SOUTHERN COMFORT. HE HAS A LARGE ORANGE JUICE.

ANNA   You like this? Hotel.

ROBERT   It's very big.

ANNA   I thought Americans like big.

HE LAUGHS

ROBERT   The taxi driver brought me here. I asked him to recommend me a hotel. And he brought me here.

ANNA   You spoke Hungarian?

ROBERT   I tried. *Can you take me to a hotel please?*

ANNA   And you're American, so he takes you to a big hotel! All the Americans come here. It's where the EU monitors used to stay. Now it's NATO people.

ROBERT   More like a dance floor than a hotel foyer.

ANNA   Of course.

ROBERT   They have dances here?

ANNA   Sure. When the EU go away; and NATO give up on us, what have we got left? A big hotel with nobody coming to stay. Birthdays. Wedding parties. Dances.

ROBERT   Right... Hey, I like Szeged, you know. Taxi brought me here, then I went walkabout. You have some really fine buildings. It's seems very elegant.

ANNA   Sure. But right now too many people. Too many Serbs. They're frightened of Milošević and terrified of NATO. So they come here. You're here at a bad time.

ROBERT   Milošević will back down. He's a bully. He always backs down.

ANNA   Maybe. When it's too late.
        silence

ROBERT   I like this city. I really want to visit that church you were telling me about. See this famous Black Madonna of Szeged. And the synagogue. How're you fixed the next couple of days? You think you could show me round a bit?

ANNA   Of course. I said I would. Your research?

ROBERT   Well, that's the excuse. Get to know the place. Talk to people. Hey, how about we have something to eat?

ANNA   Not here.

ROBERT   Whatever.

ANNA   You OK to take a taxi? There's a great fish restaurant just out of town.

ROBERT   Sounds great to me.

UNIT Four   **James watches B. dancing.**

ANNA's VOICE (on the language school tape):
The title of this unit is *És hol tanult táncolni.* And where did you learn to *dance?*
In this unit you will learn how to invite someone for a meal and to say whether something is or is not possible.

B. IS DANCING ALONE. HIS DANCE IS CONTAINED – QUIET, SLOW AND SENSUOUS.
THIS IS NOT TO ATTRACT ATTENTION BUT TO HOOK **JAMES**.
A CLASS ACT. NORMALLY HE EXPECTS BOTH MEN AND WOMEN TO WATCH HIM; BUT
NOW HE IS DANCING FOR **JAMES**.

WHEN HE IS FINISHED HE GOES TO **JAMES**.

B.   Tell me I dance fine.

JAMES   You dance beautifully.

B.   Thank you!

JAMES   You do.... You dance very beautifully... a beautiful inner stillness , a wonderful sense of control of your body.... You don't understand what I'm saying. Do you. Believe me, you're very lovely.

B. SMILES ENIGMATICALLY, LOOKING AT **JAMES**.

You deserve better than this.

B.   (AS IF WANTING, BUT NOT DARING TO BELIEVE **JAMES**)
Sure I understand. Now tell me I'm different from all the others... You going to take me some place nice?

JAMES   Would you like to eat? Go for a meal.

B.   I'm working.

JAMES   I'm asking if you would like me to buy you a meal?

B.   You should not come here so many times.

JAMES   Why not?

B.   You know.

JAMES   Come on. I'm paying.

B.   Some place nice here. I not go out here.

JAMES LOOKS QUIZZICAL

JAMES   I do have a car.

B.   We stay here. We go.

4

HE GESTURES TOWARDS A BACK ROOM

JAMES I was thinking it would be rather nice to get out of this place.

B. You want to eat there is somewhere just two streets (GESTURES OFF).   It is very good. I stay. You come back. But you can eat here also. Many things. I order champagne.

JAMES No, no. OK. Listen. Do you know who I am?

B. Is good here. Is good two streets.

JAMES I want to take you somewhere nice.

B. Not possible. I have to be here. There is a room. (HE GESTURES OFF).

JAMES I would like to take you to dinner.

B. I work. I cannot leave.

JAMES PRODUCES A WAD OF NOTES WHICH HE OFFERS TO HIM. HE IS CAREFUL NOT TO ACCEPT THEM.

 I have a man who .... I speak to him. When we come back?

JAMES Two a.m.

B. You go to the man at the door. You ask for this man (HE GIVES HIM A CARD). You speak to him. You give him money now. You give me money later. .... Yes?

JAMES If that's the way it's done.

UNIT Five   Robert and Anna in Robert's hotel bedroom.

ANNA's VOICE (on the language school tape):
 The title of this unit is *Hány éjszakára?* How long are you staying?
 In it you will learn how to ask for a bed for the night.

ANNA The mini bar. Just like you said.

ROBERT I hardly ever use it.

ANNA The man with no vices.

ROBERT No! You got me wrong there. No... I just don't drink alone... I'd never get any work done.

ANNA You work at this time of night?

ROBERT I guess it's my excuse for not doing more during the day.

ANNA You're not alone.

ROBERT Hey, I'm sorry. Jeez. What can I get you?

ANNA Johnnie Walker Black Label.

ROBERT In a mini-bar?

5

ANNA	Of course.
ROBERT	'It's an International Hotel'. Right.

HE GETS HER A MINIATURE FROM THE BAR, POURS IT FOR HER .

No Pálinka.

ANNA	(CORRECTING HIS PRONUNCIATION) Pálinka. You really like that stuff?
ROBERT	Yeah. I loved that meal, too. You make a great host, Anna. Great place. Great host. There's something about being here that feels real good. Like it feels right. And you introduce me to these things, Anna. That restaurant. The fish stew. I'd never have had that without you. The Pálinka. That stuff is real strong, isn't it. You can really taste the fruit. But, hey, the cupboard's bare!.... I guess I'll have a beer.

HE POURS HIMSELF A BUDWEISER.

SHE SITS ON THE BED

ROBERT	Egészségedre!
ANNA	Cheers....
ROBERT	Can I ask you something personal? Do you mind?
ANNA	Please.
ROBERT	Are you married?
ANNA	Me in your room?
ROBERT	I suppose.
ANNA	A birthday present (ASSUMING HE MEANS HER RING). Would you like me to be married? Would that be safer?
ROBERT	I'm not -
ANNA	Married?
ROBERT	No. But that's not what -
ANNA	Perhaps I should go -
ROBERT	You have a boyfriend?
ANNA	A man. Older than me. Disappointed?
ROBERT	Sorry.
ANNA	Why sorry? .... I don't mean to embarrass you. Shall we talk about something different? Your research? What you said in the restaurant about needing an interpreter - I'd like to do that.
ROBERT	Hell, am I so transparent. You must think I am so rude.
ANNA	No.
ROBERT	Is he much older than you?

6

ANNA   Ten years is not 'much' older.

ROBERT   No.

ANNA   He's an art dealer. He works in Budapest. We have an apartment there together. He's a very
              nice man. Very kind. You'd like him. He's very interesting to talk to.

ROBERT   Good.

ANNA   His English is very good.

ROBERT   He has a great teacher.

ANNA   Maybe.

              ALL THE FOLLOWING DIALOGUE OVERLAPS...

ROBERT   I should have asked you / before

ANNA   He has his life, I have / mine

ROBERT   It's not / that I

ANNA   We share an apartment / sometimes

ROBERT   Jeez, / I

ANNA   He is good / company

ROBERT   I —

ANNA   But he is not my / husband

ROBERT   I don't / know

ANNA   And I am not his wife....

        silence

ROBERT   Jeez, I am never stuck for words.

ANNA   Like, what are we doing here?

ROBERT   Hell, I know what we're doing here. We got talking so fast. So much. So back and forth.
              And when the taxi driver pulled up here I didn't have the sense to say - Find me some place
              else not so ... American - and so here I am. And that dance hall down there. It's Grand
              Central Station. That's no place to sit and talk. And then I say I have a mini bar. I mean that
              doesn't mean I -

ANNA   You want to talk about your research?

ROBERT   Not now. Tomorrow. Can we meet tomorrow? Can you show me the synagogue and the
              Black Madonna? Would that be possible?

ANNA   Sure... You would like me to go.

ROBERT   How are you getting home?

ANNA   How about you walk me home, and then I invite you in for a coffee and a Pálinka ...

        THEY LAUGH

ROBERT   I could call for a cab. I'll pay for it....

silence

You ever been to England? I love England. I got to go there next. Maybe you could come along? You know Dorset at all? Nobody ever goes there; and that is just so beautiful. You would love —

ANNA   I wonder.... Maybe you don't find me attractive. In which case I will need another glass of whisky to drown my sorrows.

ROBERT   Anna, you have got to be kidding.

SHE HANDS HIM HER GLASS. HE GETS HER ANOTHER MINIATURE FROM THE MINI-BAR. AND POURS HIMSELF ANOTHER BUDWEISER.

I am so -- You know I -- I thought I. I know the way I look at you. I been thinking this ... ain't right.

SHE LOOKS AT HIM, CHALLENGING HIM TO EXPLAIN HIMSELF.

It's sort of ... improper.

ANNA   If you look and mean nothing, then yes. It ain't right.

ROBERT   I remember what you wore the first class I came to.... I deliberately made mistakes so you would come over to me. You knew that.

ANNA   Of course. I know it, but I don't believe it.

ROBERT   Well, I'm telling you, you'd better believe it.

ANNA   You are very sweet.... and very strange.

ROBERT   Strange?

ANNA   Yes. Strange.

ROBERT   Why strange?

ANNA   Different.

ROBERT   How? Different?

ANNA   Not how I expect -

ROBERT   an American to be?

ANNA   Maybe....

SHE SMILES AND RAISES HER GLASS. THEY CLINK THEIR GLASSES.

Are you gay?

ROBERT LAUGHS.

ROBERT   You got to be kidding.

ANNA   Celibate?

8

ROBERT   OK, so my Masters was in Theology. That does not make me a priest!

silence

I was married.

ANNA   High School Sweetheart?

ROBERT   No.

ANNA   I'm sorry. You think I tease you?

ROBERT   I guess.

ANNA   Tell me.

ROBERT   Nothing to tell. Three years ago. We married right after I graduated. We had six months. One month of honeymoon and five months of Hell - and then she left. We had no children. And I've never seen her since.

SHE TAKES HIS HAND AND KISSES THE BACK OF IT.

ANNA   That's sad.

ROBERT   No. It was a mistake. Would have been sad as Hell to still be there. Mum warned me about her. But. Hell. You know — When you're young....

silence

ANNA   You think I should go home now...?

ROBERT   No. I think you should stay the night.

HE KISSES HER. SHE RESPONDS PASSIONATELY. THEY START TO TAKE OFF EACH OTHERS CLOTHES - SHIRT, BLOUSE, SHOES. AS HE REACHES TO UNDO HER BRA SHE STOPS HIM.

ANNA   Wait. I want you to talk to me. Tell me.

ROBERT   ?

ANNA   Talk to me. I want to hear your voice.

ROBERT   God, I want you. You are so beautiful. You are so...

ANNA   What you want.

HE IS KISSING HER NECK AND HER EARS.

Tell me.

ROBERT   I want to make love to you, Anna. My God, I haven't wanted anybody like this --

ANNA   Tell me in Hungarian.

ROBERT   You know damn well --

ANNA   Then I teach you. Tell me what you want to say. And then you learn.

ROBERT   I want to touch you all over. I want to kiss you everywhere. Every part of you. Your neck. Your ears. Your breasts. Your legs. I want to run my tongue--

ANNA	*I want to kiss you.* (H) Now you.
ROBERT	(HESITANTLY, AND UNSURE WHETHER SHE IS TRYING TO HUMILIATE HIM) *I want to kiss you... I want to kiss you.*
ANNA	*Every part of you.*
ROBERT	*Every part of you.*

SHE TURNS AWAY FROM HIM, TURNING HER BACK TO HIM. HE KISSES HER BACK, LIFTING HER HAIR AND LICKING HER NECK. HE UNDOES HER BRA.

UNIT Six   **James and B.**   **Budapest**

JAMES HAS HIS WALLET OUT. HE GIVES **B.** A SUM OF MONEY.

JAMES   This is for you. A treat. You're worth it.

TAKES THE MONEY. KISSES HIM.

ANNA's VOICE (on the language school tape):
The title of this unit is: *Hétkor ott leszek.* I'll be there at seven.
In this unit you will learn how to tell the time, how to arrange a meeting and how to express regret.

B.	For next time.
JAMES	Could we arrange a next time.
B.	Sure. Tuesday next week. Seven. In the club.
JAMES	No. That's impossible. I have meetings. How are you fixed Thursday?
B.	I don't do Thursday.
JAMES	Yeah. OK. So where can we meet?
B.	Is not allowed. Only at the club. A bit of fun. Meeting is not allowed.
JAMES	Not allowed by who?
B.	Bye-bye. I go now.
JAMES	This is crazy. Who is he to allow and not allow?
B.	(REGRETFULLY, GENTLY) It is business. You know business. He look after me.
JAMES	Look. I've never... OK. Right. I'll talk to the guy, right. Do a deal.

B. BLOWS HIM A KISS, AND LEAVES. **JAMES** ALONE.

Shit, shit, shit.

10

UNIT Seven   **Robert's hotel room.**

ANNA's VOICE (on the language school tape):
> *Unit number seven: Nadyon jól érezte magam.* Unit number seven: I had a very good time.

In it you will learn how to talk about your marital status and about transitive and intransitive verbs.

ANNA AND **ROBERT** IN BED TOGETHER

ANNA	Were you nervous?
	ROBERT LAUGHS
ROBERT	It's very sudden.
ANNA	You have been coming to my language school for three weeks now.
ROBERT	OK. A surprise then. From the moment I saw you I've known how much I've wanted you. But –
ANNA	You know how much I wanted you?
ROBERT	Have you done this before?
ANNA	Fucked other people you mean?
ROBERT	Anna!
ANNA	What?
ROBERT	I shouldn't ask.
ANNA	Why not?
ROBERT	It's not my business.
ANNA	You don't like my language?
ROBERT	No. I --
ANNA	You want to go to bed with me, and you want me to be pure.
ROBERT	No. But.
ANNA	I shock you.
ROBERT	Yeah. I guess so. I think —
ANNA	I don't meet the right kind of Hungarian men. Not in Szeged, anyway. Either they are children and they're frightened of women or they want to be Italians; but they have only the manners of Poles and Russians.
ROBERT	Hey, Anna, isn't that a bit —
ANNA	How many Hungarian men have you been to bed with?

ROBERT LAUGHS - AND THEN THEY BOTH LAUGH TOGETHER.

ROBERT	OK.

ANNA GETS UP AND GOES TO THE FRIDGE TO GET A DRINK

ANNA	Another beer?
ROBERT	*Thank you (Köszönöm)*
ANNA	Are you embarrassed?
ROBERT	A little.
ANNA	Do you want me to go home?
ROBERT	Of course I don't want you to go home.
ANNA	You don't mind no sleep then?
ROBERT	I can sleep any night.
ANNA	I'll leave early in the morning. OK?
ROBERT	Maybe stay for breakfast?

SHE SMILES AT HIM, STROKES HIS FOREHEAD AND KISSES HIM TENDERLY; AND CONTINUES TO DO SO THROUGHOUT THE FOLLOWING EXCHANGE:

ANNA	'Maybe'.... You're strange.
ROBERT	I'm sorry.
ANNA	No. I like it.
ROBERT	How am I strange?
ANNA	In bed you are ... So warm. So... Gentle.
ROBERT	It's been a long time.
ANNA	In Budapest when you talk... You talk like a library.
ROBERT	Oh. My research. Always talking.
ANNA	But now. Even now. Afterwards. You stop yourself. In your speech.
ROBERT	Do I?
ANNA	You don't like to / talk about --
ROBERT	We never talked. She didn't like it.
ANNA	But you have many lovers.
ROBERT	No.

silence

ANNA	I wanted to talk to you. And I thought you would be safe. ....
ROBERT	Safe?

ANNA	I thought you were gay.
ROBERT	Safe?
ANNA	So polite.
ROBERT	Are gay men polite?
ANNA	Some of them. The time I went to England. Everybody was so bad-tempered. Except for two men who had a bed and breakfast hotel in Brighton where I stayed for a weekend. They were very funny and very kind. Everybody else was either rude or they wanted to fuck me.
ROBERT	Am I still safe?
ANNA	I hope not.

THE SOUND OF THREE CHINOOK HELICOPTERS APPROACHING AT LOW LEVEL. BUILDS UP RAPIDLY. **ROBERT** GETS OUT OF BED, TO GO TO THE WINDOW TO SEE WHAT IT IS. ONE AFTER ANOTHER THEY PASS OVERHEAD. SHAKING THE BUILDING AS THEY GO. THE SOUND SHOULD BE BOTH RECOGNISABLY 'REAL' AND A TERRIFYING OTHER WORLDLY THREAT. AFTER THE THIRD HAS PASSED, THE SOUND FADES QUICKLY AWAY.

ANNA	NATO.
ROBERT	Will they invade?
ANNA	Who?
ROBERT	NATO.
ANNA	Maybe.
ROBERT	Will they launch a ground attack from here?
ANNA	Maybe. If they don't, Miloševic will.
ROBERT	Is that likely?

ANNA SHRUGS.

ANNA	Either way, we're fucked.
ROBERT	I don't understand.
ANNA	We're a border town. If it's not soldiers it's refugees. And if it's not refugees it's gangsters.
ROBERT	You mind if I turn on the TV?

ANNA SHRUGS. SHE'D RATHER HE DIDN'T, BUT SHE'S NOT GOING TO STOP HIM.

ANNA	NATO helicopters. They go over all the time.

ROBERT TURNS ON THE TV. IT'S A HUNGARIAN NEWSCAST.

ROBERT	I had no / idea
ANNA	Day and night. For three weeks / now
ROBERT	we were so close....

ANNA   Maybe we have breakfast here, then we go to my apartment; and you stay with me.

ROBERT   ?

ANNA   I have an apartment in Szeged.

ROBERT   What about your boyfriend?

ANNA   He stays in Budapest mostly. He hardly ever comes here. Says he doesn't care for Szeged.

ROBERT   You're talking to a jealous guy here —

ANNA   Is that a joke?

ROBERT   I'm sorry.

ANNA   Robert, I would like you to stay in my apartment... It would make me feel that you care about me. That you want to know about me

ROBERT   I would love that, Anna. I would love that.

SHE KISSES HIM. THEY ARE BOTH DISTRACTED BY THE TV.

What's she saying?

ANNA   NATO bombed the Television Centre.

ROBERT   I don't understand.

ANNA   In Belgrade last night. They bombed the TV Centre.

ROBERT   That crazy.

ANNA   Yes. It's crazy. Talk to me, Robert. Talk to me.

ROBERT TRIES TO SMILE. SHE KISSES HIM

UNIT Eight   Milan at Anna's apartment in Szeged.

THE SOUND OF A KNOCK ON THE DOOR.... THE DOORBELL RINGS.... LOUDER
KNOCKS ON THE DOOR.... THE SOUND OF KEYS. THERE ARE THREE LOCKS TO UNDO.
FINALLY THE SOUND OF DOOR OPENING.

ANNA's VOICE (on the language school tape):
          Unit Eight: I'm looking for my friend. Unit Eight: I'm looking for my friend.

THE ACTUAL SET, AS REALISED THEATRICALLY, IS MINIMAL. BUT IT REPRESENTS:
TV, SOFA-BED, SET OF GLASS SHELVES - THE ITEMS ON THESE INCLUDE ICONS IN
GILT FRAMES AND A MIRROR. ATTACHED TO THE WALL BEHIND THE SOFA-BED IS A
COLOURFUL RUG. TASTEFULLY DECORATED BUT NOT EXTRAVAGANT. A NUMBER
OF SIGNIFICANT WORKS OF ART.

THE MAN AT THE DOOR IS DRESSED IN A BRITISH ARMY FLAK JACKET. HE CARRIES A
BRITISH ARMY KIT BAG. FROM WHAT LITTLE HE SAYS IT IS NOT POSSIBLE TO
DETERMINE HIS ACCENT OR HIS NATIONALITY.

MILAN   James?   Hello....
              Anna?   Szia....
              Szia. Ani?

14

Anybody in?   (H)
Anna?   *Anybody here?*   (H)
James?

HE LOOKS AROUND FOR EVIDENCE OF WHERE ANYBODY MIGHT BE, AND WHEN THEY
MIGHT BE BACK. HE SWITCHES ON THE TELEVISION – BRIEFLY WATCHES THE
NEWSCAST THAT **ANNA** AND **ROBERT** HAVE BEEN WATCHING.

HE TURNS DOWN THE SOUND, GOES TO THE PHONE. DIALS. APPARENTLY AN
ANSWER MACHINE AT THE OTHER END. HE LEAVES A MESSAGE:

Hello. James. It's me. I'm at your apartment in Szeged. I'll see you.

PUTS THE PHONE DOWN. OPENS HIS KIT BAG. RUMMAGES AROUND AND FINDS A
BOTTLE WITH NO LABEL. SITS DOWN AND OPENS IT. TAKES A SWIG FROM THE
BOTTLE.

UNIT Nine   **Robert and Anna in the Alsóvárosi Church**

ANNA's VOICE (on the language school tape):
The title of this unit is: *Mi a panasza?*   What's wrong with you?
In this unit you will learn something of Hungary's cultural heritage.

ROBERT AND **ANNA** IN THE ALSÓVÁROSI CHURCH, SZEGED. IT IS EARLY IN THE
MORNING. **ROBERT** HAS A VIDEO CAMERA. HE IS MAKING A VIDEO OF THE CHURCH.
HE IS PUTTING A COMMENTARY TO THE IMAGES HE IS SHOOTING.

ROBERT   This is the Alsóvárosi Church. (PRONOUNCED WITH GREAT CARE)
I came here early in the morning. The church is surrounded by open space and is very
appealing. (TURNS THE CAMERA TO **ANNA**). This is Anna Kovács, my translator.

SHE TURNS TO **ROBERT**, LAUGHS AND GESTURES FOR HIM TO STOP. HE MOVES TO
HER, PUTS HIS ARM, ROUND HER. MAKES TO KISS HER.

ANNA   Not here.

ROBERT   Superstition?

ANNA   Respect.

ROBERT   I didn't know you were religious.

ANNA   I'm not.

ROBERT   Well? I only want to --

ANNA   No ... Look. See that. (SHE POINTS TO A MARKER ON A WALL AT ABOUT HEAD
HEIGHT) The high water mark of the Great Flood.

ROBERT   We must be at least half a mile from the river here....

ANNA   Yes.

ROBERT   What's the matter?

SHE SHAKES HER HEAD.

What's the matter? Have I done something? ...

ANNA   It gives me -

ROBERT   What?

ANNA   Nothing. Look. Over there. See. Your Black Madonna.

SLIGHTLY RELUCTANTLY, UNCERTAIN WHETHER HE HAS OFFENDED **ANNA**, HE LOOKS, AND GOES OVER TO LOOK AT THE ICON OF THE BLACK MADONNA, HANGING ON A WALL OF THE NAVE.

ROBERT   Extraordinary.

ANNA HANGS BACK, UNCOMFORTABLE IN THE CHURCH. **ROBERT** CONTINUES WITH HIS VIDEO

THE BLACK MADONNA (DRESSED AS THE BLACK MADONNA OF SZEGED) APPEARS. SHE SPEAKS DIRECTLY TO THE AUDIENCE WHILE **ROBERT** MAKES HIS VIDEO AND ADDS HIS COMMENTARY.

This is so much bigger than I imagined.

MADONNA   Nobody knows how old I am.

ROBERT   About four feet high and maybe two and a half feet wide.

MADONNA   Much older than Szeged's Great Flood; older even than the Ottoman occupation.

ROBERT   Quite extraordinary.

MADONNA   So, possibly as many as three hundred years old, maybe more.

ROBERT   Almost primitive in style.

MADONNA   And I used to be white.

ROBERT   But very charged.

MADONNA   I'm sure you can see I used to be white.

ROBERT   A really striking intensity.

MADONNA   You can see that, surely. As white as any Madonna.

ROBERT   (TO **ANNA**) I'm amazed this is still here.

MADONNA   Then Turks burned the Alsóvárosi Church.

ANNA   What do you mean?

ROBERT   Anywhere else in Europe and this would have been carted off to a museum.

ANNA   So we are Europe, are we?

ROBERT   Anna, are you OK?

MADONNA   The church was saved, but many of the icons were not. Me and my child.... we were saved. A brave young boy ran in through the smoke and rescued us. Too late - or just in time. So much smoke the colour of our skin turned black....

16

ROBERT	It's beautiful.
ANNA	Can we go?
ROBERT	Sure. I'd heard about this kind of thing. But, you know, here, it's ... wow...
ANNA	I'll tell you the legend.
MADONNA	So, you see, we are not really black at all. My baby and me. And the miracle is that our skin turns colour in the smoke of the fire; but the rest of the picture is unharmed. Such is the nature of religious miracles. God be praised.

UNIT Ten   **Anna's apartment in Szeged**

MILAN HAS SLEPT ON THE FLOOR. DIALS JAMES IN BUDAPEST.

MILAN	Where are you James? James. You said you'd meet me here. Come to the phone you fucker. I'm bored. I want to talk to someone. Where the fuck are you? I'm going out. I'll be back. James? James? Fuck off then.

HE PUTS THE PHONE OFF. LEAVES THE ROOM.

Unit Eleven   **James's apartment in Budapest. James discusses business with B.**

ANNA's VOICE (on the language school tape):
    Unit Eleven: 'Mennyibe Kerül?' 'How much does it cost?'
    In this unit you will learn how to compromise and strike a deal.

JAMES IS IN A SILK DRESSING GOWN. B. IS GETTING DRESSED. THROUGH THE SCENE HE CONTINUES TO DRESS. B. IS TEASING JAMES A LITTLE, BUT THERE SEEMS TO BE TENDERNESS BETWEEN THEM.

JAMES	Tell me your name.
B.	Call me what you like.
JAMES	Tell me your name. I'd like to call you by your name.
B.	What you like.
JAMES	They call you Belle.
B.	You don't say Belle. You say 'The Black One.'
JAMES	But you're not Belle.
B.	What you like.
JAMES	Are you cross?

B. CONTINUES TO DRESS.

You're cross, aren't you... I'm sorry... What do your friends call you?

B.   You call me Belle ...

JAMES   I have a Private View to go to tonight. Could you come with me do you think?

B. LAUGHS

Is that funny?   ....   I'm not ashamed of you.   ....   You stayed the night.

B.   You made the deal.

JAMES   Please.

B.   What?

JAMES GOES TO HIM AND STOPS HIM DRESSING. HOLDS HIS HANDS.

JAMES   I can't tell you how much I want you.

B. PULLS AWAY

B.   You have a woman. 'James and Anna' on your phone machine.

JAMES   Yes, yes, of course. That doesn't change anything.

B.   You see me, you pay. You pay more, you see me more. You pay a lot, I stay the night. One time in a week. No more.

JAMES   I know that. Please. Don't say things like that. I know exactly what this is all about. You're frightened of him. I understand that. But he can be bought off. Believe me.

B.   You are very sweet, Mister James.

JAMES   But you're cross with me, aren't you. I'm sorry. I understand. I'll ask for Belle.

B.   One time in a week. OK. No more.

JAMES   ... I've never been here before.

B.   You're crazy.

JAMES   I mean you and me. ... This. ... I just don't do this. Believe me.

B.   ?

JAMES   Believe me.   ... Once a week — is that what you want?

B.   What I want!

HE LAUGHS AGAIN.

JAMES   This is business, ... Belle. This is business. I want to make a deal. .... Do you understand? .... What I'm talking about is ...   Believe me, working from out of a rather seedy night club is not the best place for you. You deserve better than that. I'm not a fool. I know what we're talking about here. It's the Russian Mafia controls these clubs. I know that. And believe me I have no illusions about... Believe me, I do not want to get on the wrong side of these guys. But they do deals. That's what they do.

B.   You are a lovely man, Mister James. Very nice. Very gentle. Very good. A 'nice bed manner'. Yes?

JAMES	I shouldn't be talking to you about this. It's not something I should be bothering you with, I know. I'm sorry. If you would just introduce me to the guy. I'll talk to him.
B.	He make telephone to you. Yes. He talk to you.
JAMES	Yes, indeed. Look, I do understand what you're saying; but I don't want to do a deal without you being part of it.
B.	You make deal, Mister James. THEN you talk me if I like it.
JAMES	And suppose I make a deal with him and you don't like it. I do not want to make a deal, and then find that you just disappear.
B.	Mister James, I go now. Bye bye.
JAMES	No. Please. Wait. I just want you so fucking much.

JAMES TRIES TO KISS HIM AGAIN.

B. REACHES DOWN AND PUTS HIS HAND UNDER JAMES'S DRESSING GOWN, TAKING HOLD OF HIS COCK, SQUEEZING IT AND SLOWLY BEGINNING TO JERK HIM OFF.

B.	You want me suck you now? Then I can go?
JAMES	No ... you don't understand.
B.	No? You don't want this?
JAMES	Yes...
B.	Yes?
JAMES	Yes.
B.	That's what you want. Not me. Fuck off. I tell him what you want. He make telephone.

Unit Twelve   **Anna's apartment. Milan returns and meets Robert.**

ANNA's VOICE (on the language school tape):
The title of this unit is: *Welcoming guests*. Welcoming guests.
In this unit you will —

BUT HER VOICE IS DROWNED OUT BY THE SOUND OF HELICOPTERS FLYING OVER AT VERY LOW ALTITUDE. THE NEXT SCENE BEGINS BEFORE THE SOUND OF THE HELICOPTERS HAS FADED AWAY....

ANNA AND ROBERT ARE SITTING ON THE SOFA. THERE IS STILL SOME TENSION BETWEEN THEM.

ROBERT	Jesus, these helicopters ... Doesn't that get to you?
ANNA	Of course.
ROBERT	Sure as Hell gets to me.
ANNA	You don't want to be in Szeged?

19

ROBERT	Anna, I haven't felt like this about anyone since I. Well, shit, Anna, I haven't felt like this. It feels good to be around you. I just think it'd be better perhaps ... take time out... come back when things are... I don't mean I just get up and go. I mean you and me together. You know —
ANNA	This is my home, Robert.
ROBERT	Hell, Anna, I been reading. You know. The Rough Guide. And there's an oil field less than twenty miles from here. Is that right? Hell, we're in the front line here.

silence

ANNA	This is where I want to be.
ROBERT	Sure.
ANNA	You don't understand that do you.
ROBERT	I think / I under —
ANNA	I take you to the church. Which I hate. I hate that place.
ROBERT	You should / have said -
ANNA	And you want to go the synagogue.
ROBERT	If I'd known, I / could have —
ANNA	You want to talk to some people and then get the Hell out of it.
ROBERT	Oh come on, no. That's not what I'm saying.
ANNA	Am I just part of your research?
ROBERT	It's not just me I'm thinking of. OK I got it wrong, / but —
ANNA	You're here in my town looking after me? Is that it? You want to protect me? Get me away from this nasty place? Is that it?
ROBERT	This is crazy.
ANNA	What?
ROBERT	I want to be with you, Anna.
ANNA	But not here.
ROBERT	Yes. Here.

silence

I want to be with you. Tell me that's not crazy. What do I tell my kid brother? I just met this beautiful Hungarian woman teaching me in a language school and she said go to this town down by the Serbian border. So I did. And we had one amazing night in my hotel room. And now I want to spend the rest of my days with her in a war-zone.

ANNA	Hungary's not at war.
ROBERT	Serbia is.

silence

ANNA	Good time for your research. I'd have thought.

HE LOOKS AT HER. SMILES IN AN ATTEMPT AT RECONCILIATION. TAKES HER HAND IN HIS. KISSES HER HAND.

ROBERT	Why do you hate that church?
ANNA	I don't know. The way I was brought up I guess.
ROBERT	To hate the church?
ANNA	Is that so strange?
ROBERT	It is where I come from. Plenty of people don't have time for it; but 'hate' —
ANNA	They hated the Catholic Church. It was the Priest who informed on my father's family.
ROBERT	?
ANNA	They were taken to Belsen.
ROBERT	Oh God, / how awful —
ANNA	He survived / somehow.
ROBERT	That's a miracle.
ANNA	It was the end of the war. He was a young child.
ROBERT	I didn't realise you're Jewish.
ANNA	My father's Jewish.
ROBERT	I'm sorry.
ANNA	You're sorry. How could you know, Robert. It just makes me tense. And you think that because I say 'fuck' I'm an easy lay /
ROBERT	Hell no /
ANNA	And that it doesn't matter to me. Why should I care if you want to go home? Fuck knows Robert, but I do.... Why am I so tense? /
ROBERT	Jeez, you got every reason /
ANNA	It should be me who's sorry, Robert.
ROBERT	I don't want to go home Anna.
ANNA	Sshhh.

SHE KISSES HIM. HE RESPONDS URGENTLY. THEY START TO TAKE OFF THEIR CLOTHES.

THE SOUND OF KEYS IN THE DOOR. ANNA PULLS AWAY FROM **ROBERT**, WHO FUMBLES TO DO UP HIS SHIRT BUTTONS.

ANNA	James? James, is that you?

THE DOOR OPENS, AND **MILAN** COMES IN. HE IS SURPRISED TO FIND THEM HERE; BUT REMAINS REMARKABLY COOL.

MILAN   *Good morning. I'm looking for James.*

ANNA   *I'm sorry. James isn't here. How did you let yourself in?*

MILAN   (to Robert) *Hello.*

ROBERT   *Hello. My name's Robert.*

MILAN   American?

ROBERT   That's right.

ANNA   *How the Hell did you let yourself in?*

MILAN   *James gave me a set of keys.*

ANNA   *They're not James's to give.*

    MILAN SHRUGS.

MILAN   *He said he'd meet me here.*

ANNA   *He didn't tell me. I think you ought to leave.*

MILAN   *Am I interrupting something?*

ANNA   *I think you ought to leave. Will you please go.*

MILAN   *Ring him. I think we should ring him.*

HE PICKS UP THE PHONE AND DIALS. **ANNA** GRABS THE PHONE FROM HIM

ANNA (LEAVING A MESSAGE)   James. It's Anna. Where are you? James. ... James. If you're there come to the phone will you... James, I need to talk to you. If I don't get you on your mobile, call me back —Where were you?

MILAN TAKES THE PHONE FROM **ANNA**.

MILAN   Hello James. I am at your place in Szeged. OK? I left you messages.

ANNA GRABS THE PHONE BACK

ANNA   James.... "What's he doing here..."? You're asking me. Jesus. What is he doing here? You tell me. This is our apartment James. You can't just go giving people keys without telling me.

MILAN TAKES THE PHONE

MILAN   Hello. James. Hi. I got here a little soon.... OK.... Yes. .... OK.

HE HANDS THE PHONE BACK TO **ANNA**

ANNA   Why didn't you tell me, James? He just let himself in.... No, it's not.... When? When, James? Just tell me when.

SHE PUTS THE PHONE DOWN

    He's driving over tonight.

MILAN	*I can wait.*
ANNA	*No you cannot.*
MILAN	*That's OK. I'll stay here.*
ANNA	*It is not OK This is my apartment. Robert and I have to work.*
MILAN	*I'll be very quiet.*
ROBERT	Shall I go?
ANNA	I'm sorry Robert. I'm really sorry about this. No. Don't go. I need to sort this out. There's been a misunderstanding. He was expecting James to be here. I've told him we need to work here today. I just need to sort things out.
ROBERT	Look, why don't I go back to the hotel? We could meet up in town —
ANNA	Hang on. Just hang on for a bit. Would you mind? Look, could you make us all some coffee?
ROBERT	?
ANNA	Coffee. Could you make us all some coffee please. Do you mind?
ROBERT	Sure, but look, I don't want to cause trouble.
ANNA	There's some in the fridge.

      ROBERT GOES THROUGH TO THE KITCHEN
      (TO **MILAN**)   *What the Hell are you doing here ?*

MILAN	*It's business, Panni. I have business with James.*
ANNA	*It's not. I know it's not. You're playing some stupid bloody game. I don't want this. And don't 'Panni' me.*
MILAN	*Who's the guy?*
ANNA	*His name's Robert. He's doing some research for a PhD.*
MILAN	University... Very good. Doctor Robert. Very good.
ANNA	*He comes to the language school. I'm helping him with the language.*
MILAN	*Why Szeged?*
ANNA	*He's looking at Religion in Hungary after the Changes.*
MILAN	*Very good.* (IN A SELF-PARODYING ACCENT) I help him. Yeah?
ANNA	*Milan, I don't want you here.... I want you to leave.... This is my apartment.*
MILAN	*I have an appointment with James.*
ANNA	*Well go to bloody Budapest and see him there.*
MILAN	*You look very good, Anna. One of these men is very good for you.*
ANNA	*Milan, please. I want you to go.*

23

ROBERT RETURNS WITH A CAFETIÈRE OF COFFEE

ROBERT   *Hungarian style coffee. Very strong.*   *(H)*

FROM HERE ONWARDS (UNTIL NOTED) WHENEVER **MILAN** TALKS TO **ROBERT** HE
SPEAKS IN THE COD ACCENT AND SPEECH PATTERN THAT HE THINKS **ROBERT**
EXPECTS OF HIM.

MILAN   Very good. Anna teaches good, yeah. Good Hungarian. Shit hot, Doctor Robert.

ROBERT   *Thank you.*

MILAN   I was telling to Anna that she look very good. Yes?

ROBERT   Yes .... Jo reggelt kivanok. Lee Robert vagyok. *(Good morning, my name's Robert Lee).*

MILAN   *(Subtly mocking – but with apparent good humour)* Good morning Robert. My name is
                 Milan. My name is not James. James is in Budapest. Hello.
     silence

ANNA   Robert, I have an idea. How about you and me go down to the synagogue; see if we can
                 arrange an interview with the Rabbi?

ROBERT   Fine.

ANNA   *Milan, this is my apartment. You can leave your things. I won't touch, I won't tidy. But just*
                 get out. By the time we get back. Right. James'll be here this evening. Come back at five.

MILAN   Szia.

UNIT Thirteen   **Anna and Robert in the Synagogue.**

ANNA's VOICE (on the language school tape):
     Unit Thirteen: *Visiting a Holy Place*; Visiting a Holy Place.
     In this unit you will learn how to express appreciation and concern.

ROBERT   *(Speaks quietly into the camcorder microphone - a commentary for his video):*
                 This is the synagogue in Szeged. It was built between 1900 and 1903. People say it's one of
                 the most beautiful in Europe. Very unexpected. You stumble on it walking along a back
                 street.

ANNA   *(Translating for Robert as she reads aloud)* "The most beautiful place in the synagogue is the
                 inside of the dome, which ... symbolises the world. In the teachings of Jewish religion.... ....
                 Morality is .... There are three sides..." No... " The three ...." (three ... three) "There are
                 three aspects that ... determine morality: work, culture and good deeds."

ROBERT   Anna, this is quite magnificent. It is so beautiful.... Anna? ...

ANNA   "The 24 columns of the dome **...** symbolise.... represent the 24 hours of the day."

ROBERT   You seem ill at ease.

ANNA   I'm translating for you, Robert. I have to concentrate.

ROBERT   I'm sorry.

ANNA	"The blue glass dome gives a ... sensation of infinite space... This shows itself in ... the way that the glass, so full of stars, becomes gradually darker and darker. In the middle of this glass is the star of David. Around it the sun's rays crown the ...." I don't know this word.
ROBERT	Heavens?
ANNA	No. Not Heavens. Maybe universe.
ROBERT	Firmament.
ANNA	Yes.
ROBERT	Wow.... This is so.... **ROBERT** GAZES UP AT THE DOME

silence

Who is Milan?

ANNA	I told you. He's a business friend of James's. It's some business deal they're setting up.
ROBERT	You know him, don't you. I'm sorry. It's none of my business.
ANNA	I think you're sweet.
ROBERT	What do you mean?
ANNA	You're jealous, aren't you.
ROBERT	How can I be jealous?
ANNA	But you are. It's nice.
ROBERT	It's not nice, Anna. It is not nice. It's horrible. I hate it.
ANNA	It's sweet.
ROBERT	It is not sweet. It is very unpleasant.
ANNA	Are we having a row?

HE LAUGHS. HE REACHES TO HER AND SQUEEZES HER HAND.

"The altar's ... keystone ...?"

ROBERT	Right. Keystone.
ANNA	The keystone is made of marble from Jerusalem. The ark is made from" ... some special wood "from the banks of the Nile."
ROBERT	Acacia wood. ... This is very special, Anna. Thank you.... For bringing me here.

ROBERT LOOKS IN AWE AT THE ALTAR, BUT HE CAN'T STOP HIMSELF:

But you know him. This Milan guy. You know him, don't you.

ANNA	I know a lot of James's business associates.
ROBERT	He knows you Anna. He fancies you. Anybody can see that.
ANNA	Do you think so?

25

ROBERT	You're teasing me.
ANNA	Maybe.... It's good for you.
ROBERT	I'm sorry. I'm being unfair.
ANNA	If I'd asked you to go, and stayed in the flat with him all day - then you could be jealous... maybe. But I asked him to leave - and I came out with you. Remember: I am your translator. "The windows on the ground floor show events from the" ceremonial? special... something "year".
ROBERT	Probably liturgical.
ANNA	Liturgical year.... The ... red flower "is the symbol for sin... the white lily for the soul's purity ...."
ROBERT	I shouldn't have asked you to —
ANNA	I offered.
ROBERT	I value that.
ANNA	You wanted to know about the Changes.
ROBERT	Yeah.
ANNA	People come in from America, Germany, UK. And they change things, Robert. Things change.
ROBERT	I guess.
ANNA	My father survived Belsen; but not the Changes. And I feel guilty about it. I give him money, Robert. I look after him. But he's a drunk. He stinks. He comes to our place in Budapest ; and I don't want to open the door. I have to hold my breath. He doesn't wash.... And he makes me feel guilty. ...

silence

	When I was child he frightened me. He seemed so clumsy.... But I think he was a good man. Maybe just not very efficient. So when a big German Company buys the fruit farm he used to work on, they sacked him because he was weak and old. Who knows? Maybe he drank too much – even then. But anyway, he hasn't worked since then, and he doesn't have a pension. And when my mother died he couldn't cope. And now he's always drunk. And I feel guilty...
ROBERT	I'm sorry.
ANNA	Why are you sorry? Robert. Why are you sorry?

ANNA LEAVES

ROBERT	(*To the camcorder microphone*): As we leave the synagogue we move back into the entrance hall, where there are massive inscriptions on the side walls, listing all the Jewish population of Szeged who died at the hands of the Nazis during the nineteen forties. At each end of the hall are two large black stone coffins. I would like to stand here to let the enormity of this sink in. But Anna is keen to leave and is already outside.

UNIT Fourteen. Anna's apartment. Milan and James make their exchange.

ANNA's VOICE (on the language school tape):
Unit Fourteen: Degrees of Difficulty. Degrees of Difficulty.
In English the comparative and the superlative are marked EITHER by adding the suffixes -er and -est OR by using the words more and most. Thus: Easy, easier, easiest; or alternatively easy, more easy, most easy. Some words, however, cannot use the suffixes -er and -est. For example in English you can say more expensive, but not expensiver; most expensive, but not expensivest.

JAMES HAS BROUGHT TWO GLASSES FROM THE KITCHEN. MILAN IS WEARING HIS JEANS AND T-SHIRT. HE POURS SOME OF HIS 'HOME-MADE' FOR HIMSELF AND JAMES. WHEN ROBERT IS NOT AROUND MILAN REVERTS TO HIS NORMAL EXCELLENT ENGLISH.

MILAN   Egészségedre!

JAMES   Egészségedre! Cheers... So you managed to find me the present?

MILAN   Of course. You know me.

JAMES   I do, indeed, Milan.

MILAN HESITATES, GESTURING THAT JAMES SHOULD RECIPROCATE.

JAMES OPENS THE SUITCASE AND TAKES OUT A SMALL BUT HEAVY PACKAGE, BUT DOESN'T YET OFFER IT TO MILAN.

MILAN GOES TO HIS KIT-BAG AND TAKES OUT A PACKAGE - WHICH COULD CONTAIN A COUPLE OF BOOKS OR PERHAPS SOME VIDEO TAPES, OR MAYBE DRUGS.

JAMES HANDS MILAN HIS PACKAGE.

JAMES   Just like Christmas, eh!

MILAN   Christmas! (*A toast*)

JAMES GESTURES 'GO AHEAD. OPEN IT' - WHICH MILAN DOES. IT IS WELL WRAPPED, AND SO TAKES SOME TIME - DURING THE FOLLOWING EXCHANGE, SLOWLY AND VERY CAREFULLY, MILAN WILL REMOVE THE WAXY BROWN PAPER TO REVEAL A PRECISION TAKE-APART RIFLE WITH TELESCOPIC SIGHTS: A SNIPER'S WET DREAM.

JAMES   I've always thought Christmas is very important in families. Certainly, a big thing in our family. So many people are cynical about Christmas. I think that's such a shame. I know it's different over here. I've not spent Christmas in Hungary. I'm hoping this year that Anna will come back to Yorkshire with me....   You're not saying very much. ... Well?

MILAN   I like it.

JAMES   Right.

MILAN   The bullets?

JAMES   In the suit case.

MILAN SCREWS THE VARIOUS PARTS OF THE RIFLE TOGETHER, FINALLY FITTING A SILENCER OVER THE BARREL.

It's the business. I'm told it's the best there is. Extremely accurate and very quiet. You could shoot me, and would make less noise than opening a bottle of champagne.

27

MILAN'S ATTENTION IS ON THE RIFLE. HE DRINKS TO **JAMES**. THEY BOTH DOWN THEIR GLASS.

> And after tonight you never see me again.

MILAN NODS. **MILAN** HANDS HIM THE OTHER PACKAGE. **JAMES** MAKES NO MOVE TO UNWRAP THE PACKAGE. **MILAN** FILLS THE GLASSES AGAIN.

MILAN	To my disappearance.

THEY TOAST EACH OTHER.

MILAN	Cheers.
JAMES	Egészségedre!

MILAN NOW BEGINS TO DISMANTLE THE GUN, WRAPPING EACH PIECE CAREFULLY.

MILAN	The bullets.
JAMES	In the case.
MILAN	That was part of the deal.
JAMES	I know. They're in the case.
MILAN	It's no fucking good unless I have the bullets. I have to have the right bullets for this fucking thing.
JAMES	Milan, don't swear. Please. It's not necessary.

JAMES OPENS HIS BRIEFCASE AND TAKES OUT A SMALL, LOCKING BIBLE. **JAMES** GIVES HIM THE KEY. **MILAN** UNLOCKS IT. INSIDE THERE IS A HOLLOWED OUT SPACE CONTAINING SIX ARMOUR PIERCING BULLETS FOR THE HIGH VELOCITY RIFLE. **MILAN** ALLOWS A TINY SMILE TO CROSS HIS FACE.

> OK? .... After tomorrow we never meet again. Never. No phone. No e-mail. No contact.

MILAN	Of course. But a shame.
JAMES	Yes. I'm sure we could be very useful to each other.
MILAN	I could bring you more.
JAMES	That is very tempting, Milan. Very tempting. But I do think it is best to know when to stop.
MILAN	Yes.
JAMES	But it is a shame. You're right. I like doing business with you, Milan. You remind me of my father. Except you speak better English!
MILAN	Only six?
JAMES	'Only six'?
MILAN	Six bullets.

JAMES   Believe me, my friend, there are degrees of difficulty. Getting the gun is .... But these.... These are ... very much a specialist item. Three for practice. And three to do the job in hand. Whatever that might be.

MILAN NODS BUT DOES NOT RISE TO JAMES'S HINT. THEY SAY NOTHING FOR A WHILE, AND THEN:

MILAN   OK. You open your present now.

JAMES   No need. I trust you. I can trust you, can't I.

MILAN   Of course.

JAMES   It is what you promised me?

MILAN   Open it.

JAMES   Later.

MILAN (*Milan shrugs.*)   And how do I go across?

JAMES   Tomorrow morning. I take you to the border for six. We need to leave here by four. All the arrangements are made. Everything you need.

HE HANDS MILAN A WALLET – WHICH MILAN LOOKS AT BRIEFLY – IT CONTAINS A PASSPORT, IDENTITY CARD AND A SUBSTANTIAL AMOUNT OF MONEY.

MILAN   Good.

JAMES   So. We have a deal then?

MILAN   Yes. Very good. A deal.

THEY SHAKE HANDS AND EMBRACE, KISSING EACH OTHER ON THE CHEEKS. MILAN TAKES HIS BOTTLE AND FILLS BOTH THEIR GLASSES. OFFERS HIS GLASS FOR A TOAST. JAMES LIFTS HIS.

JAMES   To the Lost Books of the Bible...

MILAN IS SLIGHTLY PUZZLED, BUT THEY DRINK. BY NOW EACH OF THE COMPONENTS OF THE GUN IS WRAPPED, AND BACK IN THE KIT-BAG.

JAMES   Just tell me something, Milan. I'm puzzled. You don't have to answer, of course. (*Milan gestures that he should go ahead.*)   Why this (*i.e. the gun*) when I'm told you can buy a Kalashnikov in every greengrocer's shop in Novi Sad?

MILAN   Yes.

JAMES   What?

MILAN   It's true.

JAMES   OK. (*Resigned to Milan not telling him*)

MILAN   No.. I'll tell you. This is not a Kalashnikov. This is a British gun. I need to move fast. And also I don't want to go to a greengrocer's shop.

THE SOUND OF KEYS IN THE DOOR. ANNA COMES IN, FOLLOWED BY ROBERT. AT FIRST SHE SEES MILAN, BUT NOT JAMES.

ANNA   *I thought I told you to get the Hell out of here.*

29

JAMES   Anna, darling. It's alright. I said it was alright. He's with me.

UNIT Fifteen.   **Revision exercise One**

ANNA's VOICE (on the language school tape):
Revision exercise One. Revision exercise One.
In each of the following groups of sentences, try to explain which <u>two sentences</u> are most
contradictory and which make most sense.

ANNA's VOICE (on tape):   Group One:

JAMES   James is an Englishman living in Hungary.

ANNA   Anna is a Hungarian, who speaks excellent English.

B.   James only speaks Hungarian when it is absolutely necessary.

ROBERT   Anna is a strong, intelligent and independent young woman.

ANNA's VOICE (on tape):   Group Two:

ROBERT   Milan arrives in Anna's apartment wearing a British Army flak jacket.

ANNA   Milan is a Serbian who attended university in Szeged, a beautiful town in south east Hungary,
near the border with what used to be called Yugoslavia.

MILAN   Milan has travelled widely through Europe and America.

JAMES   Milan speaks English and Hungarian, but Serbian is his first language.

ANNA's VOICE (on tape):   Group Three:

ROBERT   Robert is on a trip around Europe.

MILAN   Robert's parents dislike the people they call 'University pinkos'.

ANNA   Robert's trip has been paid for by his father.

JAMES   Robert is in Europe to do research for his PhD.

ANNA's VOICE (on tape):   Group Four:

B.   Anna and James have lived together for eighteen months.

ROBERT   Anna and Robert have become close friends.

MILAN   James and Milan each have plans to give someone a special surprise.

ANNA   Anna and Milan used to know each other quite well.

UNIT Sixteen   Anna's apartment in Szeged.

ANNA's VOICE (on the language school tape):
                    Unit sixteen: 'Getting along with strangers.'   Getting along with strangers.
                    In this unit you will learn how to introduce yourself to people you have not met before.

JAMES   (TO ANNA) *Aren't you going to introduce me?* (TO ROBERT) *Or shall I? I'm James. Anna's partner.*

          ANNA IS FURIOUS WITH HIM

ANNA   *And what about you? Don't you think I'm owed an apology?*

ROBERT   *Hi. Robert. Lee Robert vagyok.*

JAMES   The American?

ROBERT   How did you guess?

ANNA   *James, can we talk?*

JAMES   *Sure. Just saying hello.* She told me a lot about you.

ROBERT   Really?

JAMES   Yes. You go to her language school, don't you. She says you're very quick on the uptake.

ROBERT   Hey. I wouldn't say I'm quick --

JAMES   Hungarian is such a fiendishly difficult language. You're the guy doing the research? Is that right?

ROBERT   Well, yeah. Trying.

JAMES   Anna keeps me well informed. Wonderful, gorgeous Anna. Don't you think. .... How was the Synagogue?

ROBERT   ?

JAMES   Milan told me that'd be where you' gone. Oh, gosh, I am sorry. Milan. Robert. Milan is a business colleague.

MILAN   Hi.

ROBERT   Anna's partner?

31

JAMES   'Partner'. So difficult to find the right word these days, don't you think? But I do think in our case it's pretty accurate.

ROBERT   You're an art dealer?

JAMES   That's right. And you're working on a PhD? You know I really admire that. You need so much stamina and determination for that kind of work. I gave up on mine. Threw it away completely. And I have so regretted it. Anna, darling, do you think you fix us all a drink? Would you mind?

ROBERT   Regretted what?

JAMES   Sorry?

ROBERT   What did you give up on?

JAMES   My PhD. "Written on the body". Bodies as performance. Self-mutilation in the name of art. That kind of thing. But at the time I was writing. Trying to write. My dissertation. It was pretty early days.

ANNA   James, can we talk?

JAMES   Sure.

ANNA   Privately.

JAMES   We have guests.

ANNA   I have a guest. You have a guest.

JAMES   Well / exactly — (so do you think you could ...)

ANNA   *I want to talk to you --*

JAMES   (To **ROBERT**) Doghouse. Hungarian means doghouse. I am sorry, Anna. (HE GOES TO HER AND TAKES HOLD OF HER HANDS)   I am so sorry about this business with the key. It's my fault. Entirely my fault. I guess I just screwed up over dates. I had no idea you were going to be needing the flat. Milan and I have a little business to do. He's only going to be here a day or two, so I said why not use the flat. / I am so sorry —

ANNA   *James, I want to talk to you.*

JAMES   So be it. So be it.

ANNA   *Now.*

        JAMES AND **ANNA** LEAVE THE ROOM.

        ANNA AND **JAMES** HAVE A HEATED ARGUMENT, BUT CANNOT BE HEARD BY **MILAN** AND **ROBERT**, NOR BY THE AUDIENCE.

        AT THE BEGINNING OF THE EXCHANGE BETWEEN **MILAN** AND **ROBERT**. **MILAN** SEEMS VERY FRIENDLY. HE DELIBERATELY PLAYS A GAME OF NOT BEING CONFIDENT WITH ENGLISH

MILAN   American?

ROBERT   Yeah.   I come from Hicksville, Montana. But that's the bad news. The good news is I got out.   I moved to New York. I work from out the Graduate Centre. You ever been to New York?

MILAN	Hicksville?
ROBERT	Hell, that's not a real place. That's a kinda name for back of beyond. You know, like, a small town in the middle of nowhere. You wouldn't have heard of it. Place called Baker.
MILAN	Baker?
ROBERT	Baker. As in bread. You know?
MILAN	This is real place? Baker?
ROBERT	Yeah. It's a town. Town I grew up. Small town. Big people. Trying to hack a living outta next to nothing. On the edge of the Badlands.
MILAN	Badlands?
ROBERT	It's a nickname. It's what the first settlers called it. What about you? You a friend of Anna?
MILAN	I am from nowhere.

ROBERT LAUGHS, TAKING THIS A JOKE

ROBERT	The Man from Nowhere! I have heard so much about you.

ROBERT LAUGHS AT HIS OWN JOKE. **MILAN** SMILES

MILAN	What are you doing here?
ROBERT	I'm researching stuff for my doctorate. I don't know if this'll make any sense to you, but –
MILAN	I know.

silence

ROBERT	What? ... What? What do you know?
MILAN	Your research. Religion and The Changes. Sounds very good. The doctorate.
ROBERT	You know about it? How do you know about it?
MILAN	Anna tells me.
ROBERT	What?
MILAN	(*slowly, searching as if to get his words right*) About your doctorate. Sounds very good.
ROBERT	Thanks. You got to find your niche. Know what I mean?
MILAN	Niche?
ROBERT	Where you fit. Yeah?
MILAN	'Niche'. Nice word.
MILAN	You want me to tell you something?
ROBERT	For sure.
MILAN	OK. I tell you. It's of good use for you I think. I tell you? ..... I can tell you some things. But first you tell me something, yeah? We make a deal? Huh?

ROBERT	You bet.
MILAN	What you do here?
ROBERT	I told you.
MILAN	Here. Not Szeged. Not Hungary. Not Eastern Europe as you call it. Here. Anna's apartment. What you do here?
ROBERT	Anna said I could stay here, and she's going to do some translating for me.
MILAN	The 'work thing'. Yes?
ROBERT	Yeah. Why? Why do you ask?
MILAN	That is what I want to know. I ask you. It is very simple.
ROBERT	It's a work thing.
MILAN	I ask you.
ROBERT	Yeah. It's a work thing.

MILAN NODS, SHRUGS SLIGHTLY. AS IF HE HAS MADE HIS ASSESSMENT.

MILAN	It is bad time, strange time to come. I think.
ROBERT	Hell, I had no idea this Kosovo thing was going to blow up. I've been in this part of the world now for two months now.
MILAN	Here? In Szeged?
ROBERT	Three weeks in Poland. A week in the Ukraine. A week in the Czech Republic. The last three weeks here. I mean no not here. Hungary. Budapest, Debrecen, Pecs. I've only actually been / here in Szeged —
MILAN	So now it has 'blown up' why you not go home? You think now it blows up, then it blows over. Yes?
ROBERT	No, no, no, no. I do not think that. I think you guys are in one Hell of a situation.
MILAN	You stick fingers in this Hell but you do nothing.
ROBERT	Heh, is that what this is all about? What am I doing here? ... You think I choose to come here at this time? ... This is when I could come.
MILAN	Us guys. We are ... of interest ... to you Doctor Robert? Yes?
ROBERT	Yeah. I guess. Yeah. That's right. What's wrong with that? Is something wrong with that?
MILAN	But your interest is for you. You take. You write. You get your doctorate. You go to conference. You make your paper. You please the professors. They give you job. You come back. You study us some more. You write some more about us. Like chimpanzees. You write about us. You do good in your job. You get tenure. Yes? Then maybe you are big expert. You come here. You give lectures about us.
ROBERT	Shit, come on man. There is really no need —
MILAN	No. No need.

ROBERT   Hell, we seem to have got off on the wrong foot. I got nothing against you. Jesus, it's only knowledge. I'm not here to exploit anybody. And look, I'm not Doctor yet. I'm not Doctor Robert

MILAN   OK. Mister Robert....'Only Knowledge'?

ROBERT   Look, there really —

MILAN   Knowledge is not exploitation?

ROBERT   I've told you —

MILAN IS IMPATIENT AND ANGRY, BUT QUIET.

MILAN   OK. Show me your bag.

ROBERT   ?

MILAN   Your suitcase. Show me.

ROBERT   Who the Hell are you to — ?

MILAN   Show me.

MILAN GOES VERY CLOSE TO HIM. SPEAKS INTO HIS FACE.

MILAN   I don't want to hurt you. I don't want to make mess. It is rude. It is not my apartment. Show me you stupid fucker. You think I'm so dumb I don't know—

ROBERT   OK. OK. It's no big deal.

ROBERT GETS HIS BACK-PACK. HE STARTS TO UNPACK IT, PUTTING HIS CLOTHES ON THE SOFA. HIS MANNER, HOWEVER, GIVES AWAY THAT HE IS TRYING TO CONCEAL SOMETHING.

MILAN   Let me help.

ROBERT   No, it's OK. I'll do it. Right.

MILAN TAKES A FIRM HOLD OF **ROBERT** BY THE THROAT. LOOKS HIM VERY CLOSELY IN THE EYE. SAYS NOTHING. **ROBERT** BACKS OFF. **MILAN** TAKES **ROBERT**'S CLOTHES OUT OF THE BACK-PACK. FINDS A PAPERBACK, A ROUGH GUIDE TO HUNGARY. IN THE PAPERBACK A FAMILY PHOTOGRAPH:

MILAN   Mum and Dad?

ROBERT   Right.

IN THE ROUGH GUIDE THERE ARE SEVERAL AIR MAIL LETTERS. **MILAN** OPENS THEM.

ROBERT   You can't do this. Those are private letters. Who the Hell do you think you are? What the Hell are you looking for? I asked you what you're looking for

AT THE BOTTOM OF THE BACK-PACK **MILAN** FINDS A MAGAZINE.

PULLS IT OUT. GAY PORN. HE BROWSES THROUGH IT.

ROBERT   Give me that.

MILAN   Nice boys. Research?

ROBERT Give me that.

MILAN So what you do here is not to fuck Anna. Yeah?

MILAN HANDS THE MAGAZINE TO **ROBERT**, WHO STUFFS IT BACK INTO THE BACK-PACK.

AS **ROBERT** STARTS TO PUT HIS CLOTHES BACK INTO THE BACK-PACK, **JAMES** AND **ANNA** COME THROUGH FROM THE KITCHEN. **ANNA** LOOKS SURPRISED BY WHAT SHE SEES.

MILAN Robert wanted to show me his family photographs.

JAMES Very nice. We thought we'd all go for a meal. How does that sound?

UNIT Seventeen **James in Anna's apartment. B. in the night-club.**

ANNA's VOICE (on the language school tape):
  The title of this unit is: *The benefit of paying cash.* The benefit of paying cash.

IN THE BAR. **B.** IS SITTING ON A BAR STOOL. HE IS VERY ANXIOUS. SOMETHING IS WRONG. HE EXPECTS SOMEBODY TO COME IN TO THE BAR; AND HAS BEEN TOLD TO WAIT....

ANNA's APARTMENT. JAMES ON HIS OWN (**ANNA**, **ROBERT** AND **MILAN** HAVE GONE DOWN TO THE CAR?). HE GETS OUT HIS MOBILE PHONE. DIALS A NUMBER. WAITS.

IN THE BAR. **B.**'s MOBILE PHONE RINGS. HE SWITCHES IT OFF WITHOUT ANSWERING IT.

ANNA's APARTMENT. JAMES LISTENING TO HIS MOBILE. HEARS IT GO TO VOICE MAIL.

  JAMES Damn. (THEN, LEAVING A MESSAGE:) Hi. This is me. I just wanted to say Hello. I know you probably won't understand this; but I'm thinking of you. Call me back if you get a chance. Miss you.

IN THE BAR. **B.** HAS A DRINK IN HIS HAND, WHICH HE SIPS NERVOUSLY. AND PICKS HIS FINGERS. NOTHING ELSE HAPPENS.

EVENTUALLY **B.** STANDS UP. AND STARTS TO WALK OUT OF THE BAR. AS HE DOES, SO HE REALISES THAT THERE IS SOMEBODY BEHIND HIM. HE STOPS AND, TERRIFIED, LOOKS HALF OVER HIS SHOULDER....

ANNA's VOICE (on the language school tape):

That is the end of Part One of your course.

You should now take a short break from your studies. But remember to listen to people speaking Hungarian, and don't be shy: whenever possible you should try out what you have learnt.

When you return, we will start Part Two – 'Finding out about the Way of Life'.

END OF PART ONE

PART TWO   FINDING OUT ABOUT THE WAY OF
                  LIFE

UNIT Eighteen   A smart Fish Restaurant in Szeged

ANNA's VOICE (on the language school tape):
          You now start Part Two of your course.
          Part Two: Finding out about the way of life.
          The title of this unit is: *Pincér!* Waiter!
          In it you will learn about Hungarian restaurants and how to say whether you like or dislike
          some food or drink.

JAMES AND ANNA SITTING TOGETHER, **ROBERT** AND **MILAN** OPPOSITE THEM. THEY
HAVE JUST FINISHED THEIR MEAL.

MILAN SAYS NOTHING. IMPASSIVE AND INSCRUTABLE FOR MOST OF THE SCENE. HE
HAS HIS KIT BAG WITH HIM. **ROBERT** VERY CONSCIOUS OF HIM.

ROBERT GETS TO HIS FEET AND TAKES HIS CAMERA FROM HIS BACK-PACK.

JAMES   No, no, no. You shouldn't take it. You have to be in the picture. If you take it, how does
               anyone know you were here?! Here, I'll do it.

ROBERT   Well... thanks.

JAMES   Are we all ready then?

          ROBERT GIVES **JAMES** THE CAMERA. THE FOLLOWING CONVERSATION TAKES PLACE
          WHILE **JAMES** IS ORGANISING THEM AT TABLE.

JAMES   Can you imagine anywhere else in the world that would be famous for floods and fish stew?
               Well, hardly famous. But that's its claim to fame.

ROBERT   That fish stew is very good. I can see a Hungarian restaurant. Szeged style. New York.
               Seattle. Could really take off.

JAMES   Anna, that's what we should do. Believe me, Robert, I have been wanting to move to New
               York for years. I tell you what, Robert. You must look us up in Budapest. Next time you're
               in town. No, I mean it. We must take you out. The opera's rather old fashioned, I grant you.
               And their so called National Theatre makes *Cats* look avant-garde. But. There is some very
               exciting stuff going on. And some of the best restaurants in Europe.

ANNA   And the worst.

JAMES   Greek, Italian, Mandarin, Vietnamese, Thai, French. You name it, they have the best. You
               think I'm joking? Believe me, Budapest is one of the world's Great Cities.

ANNA   Twenty seven Macdonald's.

JAMES   Anna, darling, you are such a cynic.

ANNA   Or is it twenty eight?

JAMES   Macdonald's are over here because the place is full of American and German tourists.

ANNA   And because Hungarians like to think they're Westerners.

ROBERT   *(at the same time as Anna)* and not all Americans like Macdonald's.

JAMES   *(to Anna)* That is true, darling. But you shouldn't be so hard on yourselves.

37

ANNA	I'm not being hard on myself. What's the point in glamourising —
ROBERT	Do you cook, Anna?
ANNA	Not if I can help it.
JAMES	She is very good, believe me.... And we are not going to argue that one now, darling. Brandy? Liqueur? Anybody?
MILAN	Whisky.
ROBERT	I'd like to try some Pálinka.
JAMES	You must be a born traveller, Robert. Pálinka. But you've got to be in the right mood for it, don't you think.
ROBERT	I've only tried it once.
JAMES	Personally I prefer the bottles you buy from someone's garage. The 'quality' kind that you get at the airport Duty Free sort of misses the point.
ANNA	James has always been intrigued by rough stuff.
JAMES	Anna, put your claws away. We're in nice company.
ROBERT	How long have you been over here?
JAMES	About three years. I used to have a little gallery in London. And we took on this Hungarian. György Nagy. Who <u>has</u> now moved to New York. And is doing very well for himself. But at that time he was based in Budapest, so I came over. Wanted to talk to him. Work on his home ground as it were. And more or less stayed ever since. Never looked back. He went West I came East. Where are you staying?
ANNA	Fortuna Panzió.
ROBERT	Not my choice. The taxi driver dumped me there.
JAMES	Anna, why don't we ask Robert if he'd like to stay in the apartment? You're very welcome. Unless, of course —
ANNA	I already did.
JAMES	Have the spare set of keys I gave to Milan. You have to be off on your travels tomorrow, don't you Milan.
MILAN	I hope.
JAMES	*(To Robert again)* You would love the place we're having the wedding party.
ROBERT	You're getting married?!

JAMES'S MOBILE PHONE RINGS.

JAMES	Excuse me.... *(To the phone)* Yes.... Hello.... *I'm in the middle of a meal with some friends....*
ANNA	You know Margit Island? In the middle of the Danube. You must know it.
JAMES	*(To the phone) I'm really sorry. This is a very bad line. I can't hear what you're saying.*
ANNA	It's very beautiful.

38

JAMES	(*To the phone*) *Look, I'm sorry. I just can't understand what you're saying.*
ANNA	You would love it, Robert.
JAMES	(*To the phone*) *Look. I'll call you back.*
ANNA	And James has arranged for the ceremony to take place in the ruins of the old church.
JAMES	(*To the phone*) *OK. OK. I understand.... Not now.*
ANNA	It is so romantic.
JAMES	(*To the phone*) *Yes. Yes. OK. Call me again in about twenty minutes.*
ANNA	Then up to Mátyás Church for a formal blessing; and back to the ruins for the party. Isn't that amazing!
ROBERT	Sounds wonderful.
JAMES	(*To the phone*) *OK. Ten minutes.*
	SWITCHES THE PHONE OFF.
ROBERT	I thought —
JAMES	I am sorry. Anna, darling, what are we doing here? We're talking weddings when we haven't ordered the drinks. Come on. Priorities.
ANNA	You're a shit sometimes.
JAMES	I am <u>the</u> shit, believe me. Believe me, Robert. She tells me. I'm sorry darling. I love you....
	ROBERT IS EMBARRASSED
ROBERT	What was this place before they turned it into a restaurant?
JAMES	We're teasing. Very anti-social. I am sorry.
ANNA	It's true.
JAMES	What?
ANNA	You're a shit. (**JAMES** KISSES HER OSTENTATIOUSLY)
JAMES	Would you like to come to the wedding? That would be so nice if you could come to the wedding. And you, Milan. It'll be a lot of fun. I promise. You must come. Both of you. It's important to us. ... Now, if you'll excuse me, I must –
	HE LEAVES THE TABLE TO MAKE HIS PHONE CALL.
ROBERT	I guess maybe I should head on back to the hotel.
ANNA	No. We'll drop you. James can drive you.
ROBERT	Hey. I don't want to be a nuisance. Anna —
ANNA	You don't want to walk through Szeged at this time of night. Not these days. Not with the so-called refugees everywhere. It used to be really quiet.
ROBERT	Bad timing, eh!

39

MILAN   He come back with us. I sleep on floor.

ANNA   Too crowded, Milan.

MILAN   No. I was very rude before. I sorry. I apologise. We have plenty talk about. Me and Robert. I help him with his research.

ROBERT   Well. I guess —

UNIT Nineteen   **James on the phone**

ANNA's VOICE (on the language school tape):
The title of this unit is: *'Kivel beszelek?'*   'Who am I speaking to?'
In it you will learn to make telephone calls and to use some of the simple every day expressions that lovers use.

JAMES IN A LIGHT THAT ISOLATES HIM. WE CANNOT HEAR THE PERSON ON THE OTHER END OF THE PHONE.

JAMES Hello....   *Yes.... Yes....*

What? When was that? ....

OK. I'll find somewhere for you...   *I promise ...*

I swear to you ....

Tell me where you are   .....

Yeah. I'll find you something....

Just get yourself to a public place. *Public....*

The opera. *Opera.* Go there now.

Yes....   I'll find you a hotel...   Yes...

I'll get a taxi meet you at the opera.

The foyer *of the opera.* The foyer. How am I to know what a fucking foyer is in Hungarian? Tickets. *Tickets.* Where you buy tickets.

As soon as I've found a hotel, I'll organise a taxi....

Yes.. yes.. yes. The taxi driver will have the money....

I am sending a fucking taxi. The taxi driver will have the money

The driver will have the money for the hotel ...

Tomorrow. *Tomorrow....*

I will come for you. Don't go out. Just wait at the hotel.

UNIT Twenty   Anna's apartment. The confrontation between Milan and Robert.

ANNA's VOICE (on the language school tape):
> *Unit Twenty: Having a drink with friends.* Having a drink with friends
> In it you will learn how to deal with the unexpected.
> ------------------------

LAUGHTER....
ANNA, JAMES, ROBERT AND MILAN ARE IN THE LIVING ROOM TOGETHER. THEY
EACH HAVE A DRINK. JAMES AND MILAN ARE SLIGHTLY DRUNK, AND LAUGHING
LOUDLY. ROBERT HAS JOINED IN – SLIGHTLY NERVOUSLY. ANNA, STONY FACED,
HAS NOTICED MILAN'S PACKAGE FOR JAMES ON THE SHELF.

JAMES   I have a very special bottle of wine for an occasion like this.

MILAN   Yes.

JAMES   Robert?

ROBERT   Sure. Thanks.

JAMES   Anna? .... Are you going to join us? .... Another?

ANNA   No.

JAMES   Oh well.... Anna, darling, I don't suppose we have any nibbles in do we? Something nice and sweet to go with a really good Tokaj?

ANNA SHRUGS.

MILAN   *Have a drink, Anna.*

ANNA   *I don't want one.*

JAMES   Shame. You're fun when you're drunk.

ANNA   *Shut up.*

MILAN GETS A BOTTLE OF 'HOME-MADE' FROM HIS KIT-BAG, AND OFFERS SOME TO
ROBERT.

ROBERT   I'd rather not, if its OK with you. My mother always told me never to mix drinks.

MILAN   Very good! But your mother she is not here tonight. So.

ANNA   *Milan, what are you playing at with that bloody stupid voice?*

MILAN IGNORES HER, POURS HIMSELF A SMALL TUMBLER, AND ONE FOR ROBERT.

MILAN   Egészségedre!

ROBERT RATHER RELUCTANTLY LIFTS HIS GLASS TO TOAST MILAN

ROBERT   Egészségedre!

MILAN DRINKS HIS DOWN IN ONE; AND ROBERT FEELS OBLIGED TO FOLLOW HIS
EXAMPLE. THE SPIRIT IS ROUGHER AND STRONGER THAN RESTAURANT PÁLINKA,
AND HE IS A BIT SHAKEN BY IT.

MILAN BEGINS TO SING TO HIMSELF — AND CONTINUES TO DO SO UNTIL AFTER
JAMES AND ANNA HAVE LEFT THE ROOM..

ANNA   You're mad. Both of you. Robert, you don't have to do this.

ROBERT   It's OK. I can look after myself.

ANNA   *Milan, you really piss me off sometimes. You know that.*

ANNA LEAVES THE ROOM IN DISGUST, HEADING FOR THE BATHROOM. AS SHE
GOES, SHE PICKS UP THE PACKAGE THAT MILAN HAS BROUGHT FOR JAMES. AS SHE
LEAVES, SHE SAYS : —

ANNA   If this is going to be boys getting drunk I'm going to have a shower.

ROBERT   Anna.

ROBERT GETS UP AND WANTS TO FOLLOW ANNA.

ANNA   Not now.

ROBERT   Anna, I just want to tell you —

ANNA   Not now.

SHE SHUTS THE DOOR BEHIND HER.
ROBERT AND MILAN IN THE ROOM ON THEIR OWN.

silence

THE SCENE SPLITS – SO THAT WE SEE JAMES IN THE KITCHEN AND MILAN /
ROBERT IN THE LOUNGE. THE THREE SCENES TAKE PLACE SIMULTANEOUSLY.
BUT WE CAN ONLY HEAR THE DIALOGUE IN ONE AT A TIME.

UNIT Twenty A (20A)

IN THE KITCHEN:
JAMES GETS A GOOD BOTTLE OF TOKAJ FROM A CUPBOARD AND FOUR TOKAJ
GLASSES. PUTS THEM ON A TRAY. IS ABOUT TO RETURN TO THE LOUNGE WHEN HE
DECIDES TO MAKE A TELEPHONE CALL WITH HIS MOBILE PHONE. HE TRIES TO DIAL
A NUMBER SEVERAL TIMES. GETS NO REPLY. HE GETS HIS FILOFAX OUT AND CHECKS
A NUMBER. DIALS AGAIN. STILL NO REPLY. LOOKS IN THE FILOFAX FOR ANOTHER
NUMBER. DIALS THAT. FINALLY HE DIALS THE HOTEL WHERE HE HAS ARRANGED
FOR B. TO STAY. THE AUDIENCE CANNOT HEAR THE CONVERSATION HE HAS WITH
THE HOTEL RECEPTIONIST; BUT IT IS EVIDENT THAT HE IS DISCONCERTED.
SOMETHING HAS
GONE WRONG.

IN THE BATHROOM:
ANNA BOLTS THE DOOR BEHIND HER. SITS ON THE LOO. UNWRAPS THE PACKAGE.
REMOVES THE BROWN PAPER WRAPPING AND SEVERAL LAYERS OF CLOTH BEFORE
SHE FINALLY GETS TO THE PAINTING THAT THE PACKAGE CONTAINS. IT IS AN ICON
OF A MADONNA AND CHILD, PAINTED ON WOOD, ABOUT EIGHT INCHES HIGH BY SIX
INCHES WIDE, IN THE STYLE OF THE ITALIAN RENAISSANCE. THE MADONNA AND
CHILD ARE BOTH BLACK. ANNA EXAMINES IT CAREFULLY. IN THE **UNIT 20A**
VERSION OF THE SCENE ANNA LOOKS AT THE PAINTING INTENTLY. SHE DOES **NOT**
MOUTH THE DIALOGUE THAT IS GIVEN TO HER IN **UNIT 20B**

IN THE LIVING ROOM:

MILAN   Anna, she is mad with us. Yes?!

   HE LAUGHS

ROBERT I guess.

MILAN   Naughty, naughty boys.

   HE LAUGHS – AND **ROBERT** FINDS HIMSELF HAVING TO JOIN IN.

MILAN   Speak Hungarian?

ROBERT A little. Very little. But I am learning. That's how I know Anna.

MILAN   I know. The language. School. I have been to America.

ROBERT Great. How d'you like it?

MILAN   Serbian?

ROBERT ?

MILAN   You speak Serbian?

ROBERT Not a word.

MILAN   Maybe I teach. Listen to me. Yes.
       My name is Milan.   (S)
       My name is Milan. Yes.

ROBERT Yes.

MILAN   Good.
       Good.   (S)

ROBERT *Good.*

MILAN   Your name is Robert. You say:
       My name is Robert. (S)   Yes. You say.

ROBERT *My name is Robert* (S) *(but pronounced and
                  remembered with difficulty)*

MILAN   Very good. Now I speak and you listen hard. OK?
       I think you're dangerous. (S)

ROBERT I don't understand. *I don't understand. I am American* (H)

MILAN   No.

ROBERT What do you mean?

MILAN   (SUDDENLY DROPPING THE PRETENCE OF THE DOGGEREL ENGLISH) I said I
       think you're dangerous.

ROBERT Me? You got to be kidding. Me? I'm dangerous to myself, sure. I know that. You know, I
       didn't even want to check in to that big International Hotel. The taxi driver took me there
       because he picked up on my accent; and Jeez —

MILAN	*I think you understand more than you pretend.* (S)
silence	
	Serbian. I think you understand more than you pretend.
ROBERT	You have got me so wrong.
MILAN	We should be friends. You and me.
ROBERT	Right.
MILAN	But no. You don't know who you are.
ROBERT	I don't get you.
MILAN	How can I know who you are — if you don't know who you fucking are.
ROBERT	Hey, I'm sorry. I am really sorry. But I just don't understand what you're getting at.
MILAN	The Language School. Yeah?
ROBERT	Jesus, I just don't... I mean what ...?
MILAN	What do you do there?
ROBERT	Jesus Christ, that's obvious isn't it. My Hungarian is shit. I need all the help I can get.
MILAN	You don't say!
ROBERT	I'm here as Anna's guest. I'm not here for you to interrogate me.
MILAN	You're doing research. But you don't ask questions.
ROBERT	I do not have to —
MILAN	You talk to Anna about her parents?
ROBERT	I don't want to impose for Christ's sake. Anna's —
MILAN	And what about me? What religion am I? Islamic? Orthodox? Atheist? Do you know? Do you care? No. Do you fuck?
ROBERT	Aw come on. / This is crap.
MILAN	You have the hots for Anna. And you have a bag / full of gay boys.
ROBERT	This is such crap.
MILAN	Who are you?
ROBERT	I do not have to listen to this.
MILAN	Is my Hungarian shit?
ROBERT	Hell, no.
MILAN	It's good, right. You know why I speak Hungarian? I came to University here in Szeged. I'm a Serbian; but I have many Hungarian friends. You know that many Hungarians live in Serbia? Your government agreed it.

ROBERT   But that was years ago. That's nothing to do with me.

MILAN   *I think you're here to cause trouble. And if that's right, then believe me, you will find trouble.*
      I promise you. (S)
      Understand?

ROBERT   No, I'm afraid not.

MILAN   *Serb?*

ROBERT   I realised that.

MILAN   *I think that the Yugoslavian War has been a terrible thing. And it is not over. First we have*
      Croatia, then Bosnia, now Kosovo. And when Kosovo is over, Macedonia. And then
      Vojvodina. And you think it's the nationalists in Serbia who are to blame.... But it's you
      Americans who bring Hungary into NATO, Americans who bomb the bridge in Novi Sad,
      Americans who block the Danube. You. Americans. You try out your weapons and then
      you're gone. I want it to be over. I want no more wars. Do you understand this? (S)
      Do you understand this?

ROBERT   No, really. Apart from the things you've taught me, absolutely nothing. Not a word.

MILAN   Nothing?

ROBERT   Well, no. Names, I know the names. Kosovo, Bosnia, Macedonia —

MILAN   Of course.... Take it off.

ROBERT   Oh come on. What the Hell is this?

MILAN   *(Pulls a knife from an inside pocket)* I want to know why you're here.

ROBERT   I've told you.   *(Milan moves the knife closer to Robert)*

MILAN   Shhh.... Take it off. *(Pinning Robert on the point of the knife)*

ROBERT, SUDDENLY VERY SCARED, TAKES OFF HIS JACKET.

      Give it to me.

ROBERT GIVES HIM THE JACKET. MILAN GOES THROUGH THE JACKET POCKETS,
FINDING A WALLET, PASSPORT AND VARIOUS BITS & PIECES - KEYS, A USED TRAIN
TICKET A FEW COINS - AND A FOLDED PIECE OF PAPER. HE UNFOLDS IT: ANNA's
HEADED PAPER FROM THE LANGUAGE SCHOOL. MILAN READS ALOUD WHAT SHE
HAD WRITTEN ON IT:

      "Kovács Anna. Budapest number: 1 - 116 – 4505. Szeged: 62 - 268 – 972.
      I'll be in Szeged from Thursday 22nd to Monday 26th. It'd be great to see you.
      Take Inter City train from Nyugati station. Call me. Szia. Anna."

      OK, Robert, so you do want to fuck Anna. Yes? Or is it the Language School? Eh? Robert?
      Which is the one you want to fuck? Anna or the Language School?

ROBERT   You're mad.

MILAN   I have a knife and you insult me.... Which of us is mad, Robert?

ROBERT   I care for Anna. I care for Anna very deeply. I didn't come here to fuck her. No. She offered
      to show me around. Yeah and we —

MILAN   You come here to fuck Anna. Yes?

ROBERT   Jeez. I'm a student. I've got nothing to do with the goddam war.

MILAN   *(At knife point)* You fuck Anna.

ROBERT   ... Yeah. We've been to bed. Yeah. Is that what you want me to say?

MILAN   ... No. ... But Anna is stupid. Anna has the eye for the main chance.

ROBERT   Believe me, I'm no —

      silence

      I'm just what I said I am.

MILAN   OK. Sure. Everything. Off.

HE GESTURES TO **ROBERT** TO TAKE OFF HIS TROUSERS. **ROBERT** IS ABOUT TO
PROTEST, BUT **MILAN** WARNS HIM NOT TO MAKE A NOISE.

UNIT Twenty B (20B)

ANNA's VOICE (on the language school tape):
      This is not an easy unit. So now we suggest you replay the tape, and watch the scene again.

THE ACTORS MOVE BACK TO THE POSITIONS THEY WERE IN AT THE POINT WHEN
ANNA HAD COMPLETED UNWRAPPING THE ICON OF THE BLACK MADONNA.

IN THE KITCHEN JAMES HAS PROBABLY REACHED THE POINT WHERE HE IS
CHECKING THROUGH HIS FILOFAX.

IN THE LIVING ROOM: **ROBERT** AND **MILAN** PROBABLY JUST BEFORE THE POINT AT
WHICH **MILAN** DROPS THE PRETENCE OF THE DOGGEREL ENGLISH.

THE FOCUS OF THE SCENE IS NOW **IN THE BATHROOM**:

ANNA IS JOINED IN THE BATHROOM BY THE ACTOR PLAYING **B.**

THE ICON EXISTS IN ITS OWN RIGHT; BUT IS ALSO PLAYED BY THE SAME ACTOR AS
PLAYS **B.**, WHO SHOULD NOT MAKE ANY EFFORT TO CONCEAL HIS IDENTITY.

ANNA   *What are you doing here?*

MADONNA   I am here.

ANNA   *You belong in church. He shouldn't have brought you here.*

MADONNA   I bring trouble. Is that it?

ANNA   *We're not Christians.*

MADONNA   Robert is.

ANNA   *My mother hated Christians.*

MADONNA   Not all Christians are bad.

ANNA   *I didn't say they were. I said my mother —*

MADONNA	Robert's parents are Christians. His father is paying for Robert's trip round Europe. Did he tell you that?
ANNA	*I like Robert.*
MADONNA	He's a nice guy.
ANNA	*What do you know about Robert?*
MADONNA	They want the best for him. They want for him what they never had. And they think that coming to Europe will make him a good Christian. Help him get over his bad marriage. Get those pinko university ideas out of his head.
ANNA	*That's his parents.*
MADONNA	And you ... are getting married to James in Mátyás Church. Why did you lie to Robert?
ANNA	*I did not lie to Robert.*
MADONNA	You did not tell him the truth.
ANNA	*He asked if I was married. I'm not.*
MADONNA	And having your wedding party in the ruins of the Dominican Church on Margit Island.
ANNA	So? .. So? ...
MADONNA	That's difficult.
ANNA	*What is?*
MADONNA	Difficult to arrange.
ANNA	*James likes to impress.*
MADONNA	He cares about you Anna.
ANNA	*You think I don't know that. Why the fuck are you telling me this?*
MADONNA	Maybe this is why I'm here. To help to make arrangements. Grease the wheels.
ANNA	*I do not believe this. I do not want any part of all this.*
MADONNA	Not so easy though. You are part of it. You knew about James. You knew what he was about when you agreed to marry him.
ANNA	*Who says I'm going to fucking marry him anyway?*
MADONNA	He does. He's very proud of it Getting married is how he stops us getting too serious.
ANNA	'Us'?
MADONNA	His pick ups.
ANNA	*And are you one of his pick ups?*
MADONNA	For the moment. While I grease the wheels.
ANNA	*I don't want this. I don't want any part of it.*
MADONNA	You are part of it, Anna. From the moment you met James you've been part of it.

47

ANNA	*No, I bloody wasn't.*
MADONNA	It was a deal. You've always known.... The language school. It's money laundering. You know that. Laundering? You know that word?
ANNA	That's a lie. *You think I'm stupid?*
MADONNA	Not stupid, no. But I know what troubles you.
ANNA	You're a smug fuck.
MADONNA	He teaches you good English.
ANNA	*Why does he have to bring you here?*
MADONNA	I'm part of his work. I am his work. And Milan. And you. We're all part of it. It all balances, Anna. Everything balances. Dirty money, clean money; Robert for you, me for him. The school for / you, the –
ANNA	*I could destroy you.*
MADONNA	You could. Easy. But you'd lose everything. And what about your father?
ANNA	*I'm going to have a shower.*

UNIT Twenty C (20C)

THE SCENE AGAIN REPLAYS THE EARLIER ACTION (**ANNA** SITTING ON THE LOO – LOOKING AT THE ICON OF THE BLACK MADONNA – **JAMES** IN THE KITCHEN, TRYING TO MAKE HIS PHONE CALL) BUT FROM FURTHER ON IN EACH OF THE SCENES, SO THAT THE POINT THAT IS REACHED AT THE END OF THIS IS THE POINT AT WHICH **ANNA** DECIDES TO HAVE A SHOWER.

MILAN GESTURES TO **ROBERT** TO TAKE OFF HIS TROUSERS. **ROBERT** IS ABOUT TO PROTEST, BUT **MILAN** WARNS HIM NOT TO MAKE A NOISE.

ROBERT	*(In an urgent whisper)* What are you looking for? *What are you looking for?*
MILAN	I want to know who you are.
	silence

THROUGHOUT THE FOLLOWING, **ROBERT** UNDRESSES TO HIS UNDERPANTS.

	You think I'm mad, yeah? Yeah? Is that what you think?
ROBERT	No. No. I don't know. I do not understand what this is about.
MILAN	OK. Maybe I am. But I understand my madness. I understand Serbian madness. Your problem is that you don't understand the American madness.
ROBERT	?
MILAN	America is like a child that gets bored if it doesn't have a fight. A Cold War that bankrupts the Socialist Alliance. And America wins. A little war here and there. And America wins. A Big War in the Gulf to save Democracy. But confusing, Mister Robert, because Kuwait and Saudi-Arabia are just as bad as Iraq. But America wins, so it's a Good War.... But the Balkan

Wars ... I'm confused. Because you can't win. You can drive us out of our homes, you can kill my mother and father in one of your precision bombing raids, you can mess up so bad that a man like my brother, Stevan, gets drafted and sent to Kosovo, where he gets shot in the back by an Albanian sniper.

ROBERT   Hey, I'm real / sorry to hear that —

MILAN   But you can't win..... Many Serbs are frightened. They fear that people want to take their land. They're like dogs... in corners. When dogs are frightened, they fight. And this means that our so-called leaders see easy ways to stay in power. They growl a bit, they snarl, they show people how tough they are. When people are frightened, they like their leaders to do that. I understand. I don't like it. But I understand.... What I don't understand is the American madness. In the Gulf, yes. Everyone knows it's oil. In South America, Panama, Cuba? .... well, I don't want to be rude about Uncle Sam; but ... I understand. But here? Why is America so frightened of the Balkans? Miloševic is not a nice guy. I know that. But America is not frightened of him. And until America started bombing Serbia most of my friends would happily put a bullet in him. Why spend billions of dollars bombing Kosovo and Serbia when / you —?

ROBERT   Because something has to be done. You know that.

MILAN   Something only has to be done, Mister Robert, when people are frightened.

ROBERT   That is simply not the case. You underestimate the / strength of feeling in —

MILAN   So I think America must want the Balkans to be unstable.... / Why is this do you think?

ROBERT   That is crazy. That / is just so

MILAN   Yes. Of course. It is crazy.

ROBERT   I don't think you / even begin to —

MILAN   So America has people in Serbia who ... encourage the / leaders.

ROBERT   This is—

MILAN   You call them advisers I think. Yes? America advises everyone. Gorbachev, Pinochet. They had good American advisers. Yes?

ROBERT   Christ, Gorbachev didn't have American advisers.

MILAN   No? You don't think so?

ROBERT   No, I do not.

MILAN   OK. OK then. This Balkan war. Who do you fight for? Albanian drug dealers. Traffickers in child prostitutes. Who are your good friends and allies? You don't fight this war for Kosovo. You don't fight it for good people in Serbia. And you don't fight it to destroy Miloševic because people who used to hate Miloševic say 'No, Miloševic is not the problem. America is the problem. It's the Americans we hate.' And Americans don't like to be hated. So I think what is going on here? Why do we get ourselves into this mess in Kosovo? Because there are people sitting in comfortable chairs who are giving good advice. And why this advice? What is America frightened of? I'll tell you. Europe.... America does not like the European Union.

ROBERT   Aw come on. You have got to be kidding.

  silence

MILAN   No.... Now. Tell me why you go to the Language School.

49

ROBERT	To learn Hungarian for Christ's sake.
MILAN	But you don't. You're fucking useless at Hungarian.
ROBERT	Hungarian's a very difficult language.
MILAN	But you're a very intelligent guy.

silence

ROBERT   Can I get dressed now?

silence

MILAN   Take them off.

ROBERT   What?

MILAN   Take them off.

MILAN GOES TO **ROBERT** – PUTS THE KNIFE POINT ON HIS THROAT AND GESTURES TO HIM TO DROP HIS PANTS.

Touch your toes.

ROBERT   For God's sake.

MILAN   Yeah. That's right. It's called a search, Robert. You have this in America? Maybe your lover will come and rescue you? Yeah? You know what? I don't give a shit.

UNIT Twenty D (20D)

THE KITCHEN:

JAMES HAS HIS HEAD IN HIS HANDS. HE IS CLOSE TO DESPAIR. HE DIALS ANOTHER NUMBER ON HIS MOBILE.

JAMES   *Hello.... My name is Hart. James Hart. I'm trying to get in touch with a friend of mine. I booked a room for him in my name....*
Yes I know I did...
(IMPATIENT) Well, I'm ringing again.....
Will you call me if he books in?

50

UNIT Twenty One   Robert and The Black Madonna in the bathroom

ANNA's VOICE (on the language school tape):
> The title of this unit is '*Milyen emberek voltak a szülei?.*' 'What were your parents like?' In it you will learn more about how to talk of the past.

Anna has finished her shower, and now Robert has gone to the bathroom. When Hungarians speak of the bathroom they mean the room in which there is a bath. In America, however, this is not always the case. If you ask to visit the 'bathroom' in America you may well find that there is no bath in the room. But on this occasion Robert has gone to the bathroom because it has been a very hot day and he feels dirty.

ROBERT IS HALF UNDRESSED. BUT HE IS DISTRACTED BY THE SIGHT OF THE ICON OF THE BLACK MADONNA. HE PICKS UP THE ICON AND LOOKS AT IT IN DISBELIEF.

ROBERT My God, where the Hell d'they get this from?

MADONNA Milan rescued me.

ROBERT Jesus... This is the real thing... This is ...

MADONNA Black.... Enjoy looking.

ROBERT We gotta get this out of here.

MADONNA Rescue me. Protect me, big American. Take me away, keep me safe. Show me off. Look at me. Marvel at my strangeness. At my unfathomable history. Or maybe take me back ... Bosnia. Where I belong. Wherever that is. I have a big family. I am an illegal alien.

ROBERT This isn't safe ....

MADONNA Not safe for you.

ROBERT Milan -

MADONNA Milan will kill you if you try to stop him. They all use me. That's what I'm for.

ROBERT There is such purity about —

MADONNA What is that? Purity?

ROBERT I don't mean in a moral sense.

MADONNA Ahh. The beauty of form. A Platonic sense then? An aesthetic sense? Of course. A purity of form — unsullied by my personal history, by the ways I have been abused, by the stories that have been told about me, by the sacrifices I have inspired. 'Purity'.

ROBERT You are beautiful.

MADONNA Thank you. ... Beautiful? To be treasured for my beauty. Because I am young, because my body is glowing with health. Do you know the stories about my colour?

ROBERT The fire. Yeah. The little kid rescuing you. Yeah.

MADONNA You think that what I want is to nurture my child, for my child to thrive - because he is the son of God, and because he is my son; because I am the perfect beautiful mother. But imagine... that when you look at my smile, my beatific smile, what you see is the pleasure he gives me.

HE TAKES THE WHITE SHROUD IN WHICH HE IS DRESSED AND EXPOSES A NIPPLE.
TAKES UP THE POSE OF A MADONNA WITH CHILD.

That when he sucks on me, and I give him milk, I have the pleasure.... Is that impure? .... Or maybe I could suck on you Robert? You like that? What would your mother and father think of that, Robert?

ROBERT   This is dangerous.

MADONNA   'Not safe'. Not safe at all. Men are always trying to keep me safe. They fight for me, Robert. Would you?

ROBERT   What?

MADONNA   Lay down your life for me?

ROBERT   I'm a pacifist.

MADONNA   So you would, then?

ROBERT   I would do what I could to prevent any harm coming to you.

MADONNA   Do you think I like that? The sacrifices men make! — for the Homeland, the Nation, for Revenge, for Faith. And, of course, for my Blessed Purity. In the knowledge that I will stay at home and gird their children around me and succour them — even when we are all made as homeless as Roma.... A pacifist? What does that mean? I have always wondered.

ROBERT   Who are Roma?

MADONNA   Gypsies. You don't have them in America.

UNIT Twenty Two   **Anna's Apartment.**

ANNA's VOICE (on the language school tape):
'*Hová Menjünk*' 'Where shall we go?'
By now you should be quite confident with your Hungarian. But you will also need to be brave and trust to your instincts.

MILAN, ROBERT, ANNA AND JAMES ARE ALL IN THE LOUNGE.
JAMES IS VERY DISTRACTED; AND PAYS LITTLE ATTENTION TO THE OTHERS.
ROBERT IS DRESSED, BUT STILL VERY WARY OF MILAN. A LONG SILENCE. JAMES IS
HOLDING THE PACKAGE WITH THE BLACK MADONNA IN IT. AT THE BEGINNING OF
THE SCENE THE ACTOR EMBODYING THE BLACK MADONNA STANDS BEHIND HIM
AND SPEAKS TO HIM QUIETLY — UNHEARD BY ANY OF THE OTHERS.

MADONNA   Do you know where I come from?   ... You don't really believe Milan, do you. But you'll have to tell people something. Unless you plan to get rid of me very quickly.

JAMES   I have no intention of doing that.

MADONNA   Take me to New York, is that it? Use me like you use Anna in Hungary. Not so much a Trophy as a visa....   And what if I were damaged in some way?

JAMES   Believe me — I'm going to keep you very safe.

MADONNA   Why?

52

JAMES   Does it matter?

MADONNA   It matters to Anna.   You think you can keep me safe?

ANNA   *I don't want you around, Milan.*   (H)

MILAN   *I can explain.*   (H)

MADONNA   I don't think you can. I don't think you want me at all.

ANNA   *I don't want you to.*   (H)

JAMES   That is so absurd.

MADONNA   I think you want to show others what interesting taste you have.

JAMES   And what do you want?

MADONNA   I'm allowed feelings, am I?

JAMES   Of course.

MADONNA   I think not. I'm an icon. How can an icon have feelings? I'm mysterious. That I come
                 looking serenely beautiful from some God-forsaken province of a former socialist country —
                 it all adds to the charm. Does it not? And my slight air of disdain — makes me nothing if not
                 exotic. Written on the body. Your stories. My body.

ANNA   (SHOUTING AT **JAMES**)   I've *had enough of this.   James, I don't want Milan here...
                 I've told you Milan. I do not want you here. (H)*

ROBERT   (IGNORED BY **MILAN** – SO **MILAN** SPEAKS OVER WHAT **ROBERT** SAYS) Anna,
                 do you have any idea of what these two are up to?
                                                                }- simultaneously
MILAN   *This has nothing to do with 'us'. Nothing to do with you and me. This is business with James.
                 (H)*

ANNA   James. Will you speak to him?

           JAMES PUTS THE PACKAGE DOWN. AS HE DOES SO THE BLACK MADONNA LEAVES.

JAMES   Look Anna, it's just tonight. Why don't I drive you and Robert to the hotel and we can sort
                 all this out tomorrow?

MILAN   NO! They are not to go.
                                                     }- simultaneously
ANNA   *I do not want to go.*   (H)

ROBERT   (AGAIN, **MILAN** IGNORES **ROBERT** AND TALKS OVER HIM)
                 Have you seen that icon? That's what they're trading, Anna.
                                                                      }- simultaneously
MILAN   *They have to stay here until after I have got across the border.*   *(H)*
                 I do not trust / the American.   *(H)*

ANNA   *This is my / apartment.*   *(H)*

JAMES   Milan, you're completely paranoid.

ANNA   *Who the Hell are you to tell us whether we can go or not?*   *(H)*

ROBERT   Can I say / something here?

MILAN *I didn't want to come here, Panni. I know it upsets you.* *(H)*

ANNA *Don't Panni me.* *(H)*

JAMES I have to make a phone call.

HE TAKES HIS GLASS OF WINE, GOES TO THE KITCHEN AND SHUTS THE DOOR BEHIND HIM. **ANNA** AND **MILAN** TALK IN HUNGARIAN – PARTLY AS A MEANS OF PREVENTING **ROBERT** FROM UNDERSTANDING WHAT THEY ARE SAYING, AND PARTLY AS A RECOLLECTION OF INTIMACY..

MILAN *I'm not chasing you. I'm not following you. I promise. James said you weren't going to be here.* *(H)*

ANNA *It's over, Milan. It's been over for years. Why do you keep doing this? (H)*

MILAN *I'm not doing it.* *(H)*

ANNA *You're here. ....* *(H)*

TWO CHINOOK HELICOPTERS FLY OVERHEAD, THEIR ROTOR BLADES THUMPING SO LOUDLY THAT GLASSES AND ORNAMENTS SHAKE. AS THEY FLY AWAY, ...

MILAN *My parents are both dead.* *(S-C)*

  silence

ANNA *When?* *(S-C)*

MILAN *The Nato bombing.* *(H)*

  silence

ANNA *I'm sorry.* *(S-C)*

MILAN *Stevan is in Kosovo.* *(S-C)*

ANNA *Your brother? I thought he was at University.* *(S-C)*

MILAN *He was forced to go to Kosovo.* *(S-C)*

  silence (AS LONG AS IT CAN BE HELD)

ANNA *I'm sorry, Milan.* *(S-C)*

SHE GOES TO HIM, TAKES HIS HANDS AND THEN TAKES HIM IN HER ARMS.

  I'm sorry *(S-C).*

  silence

  What's going on, Milan? ... Please....
  You promised you'd not try to see me again. (H)

MILAN *Trading ... I'm doing what's right, Ani. I go tomorrow. You won't see me again. I promise*
    (H).

ANNA *The icon?* *(H)*

MILAN *Of course.* *(H)*

ANNA	*You shouldn't go back, Milan. You should stay here. At least until the war's over.*
	(S-C)
MILAN	*No. I have to go back. It's alright. I'm safe. I'm not a hot-head. I am not Stevan.*
	(H)

silence

ROBERT	Anna, can we go?
ANNA	I don't know. Maybe it's best we stay for a while.
ROBERT	Would you mind / telling me —

JAMES COMES BACK IN.

JAMES	I have to go back to Budapest.
MILAN	You have to take me to the border.
JAMES	Anna can take you.
MILAN	No.
JAMES	OK. OK. I'll take you now.
MILAN	You said get to the border for six.
JAMES	I know what I said. Change of plan. I'll take you now.
ANNA	*Milan, you'll get killed.*
	(S-C)
MILAN	*You said you had everything arranged for six.*
	(H)
ROBERT	At least tell me where the icon came from.
JAMES	I have to go, Milan. I'll call the guy. We'll meet him. You'll be fine.
ROBERT	The icon. The Black Madonna.
JAMES	I bought it. That's what I do, Robert. I'm an art dealer. *(*AND THEN TO **MILAN***)* Now are you going to get your act together and are we going to get moving, or am I going to leave you here to sort yourself out?
ANNA	Why such a rush, James?
MILAN	No. Not yet. We agreed. We leave at four in the morning. You said.
JAMES	I have to go now.

BY NOW **JAMES** IS ON HIS FEET. GETTING HIS COAT.

	Milan. I'm leaving. Either you come with me and we meet the guy; or you sort yourself out. You want to stay. I'll give you the phone number. OK?
MILAN	No. You take me.

JAMES PUTS ON HIS COAT. **MILAN** STANDS. PLACES HIMSELF BETWEEN **JAMES** AND THE DOOR.

JAMES	Milan, I have to go.

EYEBALL TO EYEBALL

JAMES MAKES TO MOVE ROUND **MILAN**.

MILAN PUSHES HIM VIOLENTLY BACK. HE FALLS.

ANNA .   Milan.

JAMES   Oh for goodness sake. This is so childish.

MILAN   Get up.

JAMES GETS UP, VERY SHAKEN. **MILAN** THEN SAYS VERY QUIETLY:

ANNA   Don't hurt him.

MILAN   You know why I don't break your jaw? ... Because you are going to keep the deal. OK?

JAMES   I guess I was a bit impatient.

MILAN   I know.

ANNA   Are you alright?   **JAMES** NODS

           silence

JAMES   The icon? You know what it is then? She's beautiful, isn't she. Don't you think?

ROBERT   Yes, I do.

JAMES   Very, very beautiful. You know about Black Madonnas?

ROBERT   A bit. Anna showed me the one at the church in Szeged.

JAMES   Of course. That's why you're here, isn't it. You've seen the ones in London, have you? Our
                Lady of Walsingham?

ROBERT ISN'T SURE WHETHER HE'S TRYING TO CATCH HIM OUT. HE SHAKES HIS
HEAD.

                There's one in Willesden. How well do you know London?

ROBERT   OK. I don't know Willesden.

JAMES   Bit off the tourist trail. You should make a pilgrimage. Not exactly glamorous, I confess.
                Where does ours come from, Milan?

MILAN   Bosnia.

JAMES   There's a very famous one in Poland. But I've always found her rather ugly.

ROBERT   Milan stole it from a church?

JAMES   No. No. No. Milan is not a thief. Milan's an honest chap. We struck a deal. Milan protected
                her when things were pretty grim in Bosnia – and he's been looking after her ever since. I
                just thought that what with NATO playing war-games it was time to get her into safekeeping
                ... Snatch her from the war zone.

ROBERT   But you're making money on it?

JAMES	Does that offend you? If Milan hadn't got hold of her, then she would have gone up in smoke when the church was burnt down. And now I'm looking after her. You have to remember that in this part of the world being black doesn't get you much appreciation. Did Anna tell you about the local legend?
ROBERT	I read about it.
JAMES	How it used to be a white Madonna. Then at the time of the Ottoman invasion the local people take it from the church, they wrap it up carefully and then they bury it in the ground. When the Turks have gone they go to dig it up; and there it is, perfect, except that the Madonna has turned black. Is this a miracle? Oh yes, it's a miracle it survived a hundred years under ground not eaten by worms. But no: this is The Madonna, she survived, she lived. A sign to the people that they too will survive, they may be darkened by the invasions, but they will survive. Never mind that there are black Madonnas all over Eastern Europe.
ROBERT	The legend I heard was a bit different.
JAMES	The fire legend? ... Same legend, different story. It doesn't enter the heads of these stupid bloody bigots that their precious Madonna might have been black. It doesn't occur to them that coming from the Middle East, the mother of Jesus might just have had dark skin. There's only one group that gets a worse deal than gypsies in Hungary - that's blacks. They can worship the Madonna because she's just got a bit dirty while she was in hibernation. That's OK. Well I think that doing the right thing sometimes means getting your hands dirty. And I'm not going to sentimentalise it. ... Don't get sentimental Robert.

ANNA STARTS TO CLAP IN APPLAUSE.

ANNA	James, you are such a bullshitter —

THE DOOR BELL RINGS, AND THEN AN INCREASINGLY URGENT BANGING ON THE DOOR.

EVERYBODY STOPS. **JAMES** FRIGHTENED THAT IT MIGHT BE THE MAFIA, **MILAN** THAT IT MIGHT BE 'THE AUTHORITIES'. ANNA FEARS IT IS HER FATHER. ANNA MOVES TOWARDS THE DOOR. MILAN SHAKES HIS HEAD AND GESTURES THAT SHE SHOULD NOT OPEN THE DOOR AND THAT THEY SHOULD ALL BE SILENT.

UNIT Twenty Three.   **Anna's Apartment in Szeged. Finale.**

ANNA's VOICE (on the language school tape):
    Unit Twenty Three: 'Szeretsz engem?' Do you love me?
    In this unit you will learn how to:
    • tell somebody what to do or what not to do
    • invite and make suggestions
    • explain why you have chosen to learn Hungarian

THE BELL RINGS AGAIN. MORE KNOCKING.

MILAN OPENS HIS KIT-BAG AND, TO **ROBERT**'S ASTONISHMENT, TAKES OUT A HANDGUN AND SHOULDER HOLSTER (NOT THE SNIPER'S RIFLE THAT HE HAS TRADED WITH **JAMES**). HE PUTS ON THE HOLSTER AND THEN HIS JACKET, SITS DOWN, PLACES THE GUN UNDER THE FLAP OF THE JACKET AND NODS ('OK, OPEN IT IF YOU LIKE').

THE BELL RINGS AGAIN; FOLLOWED BY LOUD, URGENT KNOCKING.

FROM OUTSIDE CAN BE HEARD:

B.	James? ... James...

JAMES   Oh my God.

JAMES RUSHES TO THE DOOR. OPENS IT.
B. IS STANDING THERE. HIS FACE IS A MESS. HIS CLOTHES TORN AND FILTHY. HE IS
LUCKY TO HAVE SURVIVED THE BEATING HE HAS BEEN GIVEN. ONE EYE
COMPLETELY CLOSED AND BLEEDING. HIS NOSE BROKEN. HIS WORKING DAYS ARE
OVER.

JAMES   Oh my God.

MILAN   *James, what the fuck is going on here?*

JAMES   Your face.

MILAN   *We're doing business. Send him away.*

JAMES   The state of your face.

MILAN   *You promised me we would be alone. / Send him away*

JAMES   How can I send him away?

ANNA   What the Hell is going on? Who is this?

JAMES Anna. Please.

JAMES GOES TO TAKES B's HEAD IN HIS ARMS, TO COMFORT HIM.

Oh my God, this is terrible.

ANNA   *What the Hell is this?* What the fuck is this, James?

B PULLS AWAY FROM JAMES.

B.   *No. Don't touch me.*

ANNA   Some kind of refugee centre?

JAMES   Anna, I don't believe you sometimes. I do not believe you. I do not fucking believe you.

ANNA   Who is he?

B.   *Why not ask me? Stupid fucking bitch. I may be black.   But I can speak. I'm here because your Sugar Daddy Englishman asked me to come.*

ANNA   Get him out.

B.   *(To James)*   You said 'Any time'.

JAMES   *(To B.)* You need a bath and some food.

ANNA   What?

JAMES   *(To B.)* I'll run you a bath and find you some clean clothes.

ANNA   *What?*

JAMES   *(To B.)* I've been trying to ring you. I've been trying to get in touch with the man.

ANNA   *What?*

JAMES	(*To B.*) Everywhere. I've been trying bloody everywhere.
ANNA	I'll go down to local radio and get Ilona to put out message shall I? Refugees welcome. Bring your homeless to Anna's. What is it next? Stray dogs?

HE IS ABOUT TO SLAP HER, BUT HE RESTRAINS HIMSELF.

ANNA	*Don't you ever even touch me like that.*
JAMES	(*To Anna*) Go to the hotel then. Go on. Stay with the American.
ANNA	That's what you want. Get me out of the way.
JAMES	Anna, if you've got problems / with what –

ROBERT FINDS IT DIFFICULT TO TAKE HIS EYES OFF **B**. APPALLED, FRIGHTENED, BUT ALSO EXCITED — SLIGHTLY HYPERACTIVE, ALMOST LIKE A CHILD.

MILAN PRODUCES HIS HANDGUN FROM A CONCEALED SHOULDER HOLSTER — BENEATH THE FLAP OF HIS JACKET.

ROBERT	Milan, no.

ROBERT LOOKS AS IF HE IS GOING TO TRY TO DISARM **MILAN**.

MILAN HITS HIM ACROSS THE FACE WITH THE GUN. **ROBERT** SCREAMS IN PAIN AND FALLS BACK....

THE SUDDEN VIOLENCE SHOCKS EVERYONE.

silence

JAMES	*That is not necessary, Milan.*
MILAN	Who is he, James?
ANNA	*Put that gun away.*
MILAN	*Don't tell me what to do. I'm fed up with being told what to do. Don't get in the way, Anna.*
ROBERT	What's he saying?
ANNA	*What the Hell do you mean. Me get in your way?*
JAMES	*Milan, put the gun down. Anna's right.*
MILAN	*What the fuck are you doing with these guys, Anna?*
ROBERT	What's he saying?
MILAN	Ask me, Robert. I'll tell you what I'm saying.
ANNA	*I'm getting on with my life, Milan.*
MILAN	Ask me then. Or doesn't the big tough All American Boy want to talk to the dirty Balkan thug? Ask me, you fucking heap of mother-fucking shit. Ask me.
ANNA	*Milan, please.*
MILAN	Come on hero boy. Show Anna what it is to be an American.

JAMES	Milan, cool it.
MILAN	Fuck off. Ask me. I tell you. I thought Anna taught you Hungarian. I thought that's why you're here with her. So you can learn Hungarian. Isn't she supposed to be your translator. Teacher? Translator?
ROBERT	Look, I don't know what it is with you, Milan – but I am not fighting in Kosovo. And you know damn well why NATO is fighting in / Kosovo.
MILAN	NATO is not fighting in Kosovo. NATO is dropping bombs on Kosovo and Serbia.
ROBERT	NATO is fighting because your Serb army is burning thousands of innocent people out of their homes.
MILAN	You think I like that? You think my brother wanted to do that?
ANNA	*Milan, give me the gun. Please.*
MILAN	You think I like that?
ANNA	Robert, move away.
MILAN	But you don't see NATO dropping bombs on America because some renegade American agent organises the burning of Colombian villages.

JAMES HAS BEEN TRYING TO COMFORT **B.**   **MILAN** IS STILL HOLDING HIS GUN, ALTHOUGH WAVING IT AROUND LESS THAN HE HAD BEEN. **ANNA** GOES TO HIM, STANDS BY HIM.

ANNA	*Please, Milan. Let me have the gun.*

AFTER A FEW MOMENTS' DELIBERATION, **MILAN** GIVES THE GUN TO **ANNA**.

ANNA	Thank you. James, I'll get some disinfectant. His face needs cleaning up.

ANNA MAKES TO GO INTO THE KITCHEN TO GET A BOWL AND DISINFECTANT FOR **JAMES** AND **B.** BUT **MILAN** GRABS HER BY THE ARM AS SHE MAKES TO GO PAST HIM.

MILAN (QUIETLY) *Why do you go with this guy?*

ANNA	*Because I wanted to get to America, Milan. I want to get away from this. Because of my father. Because I want to get him out of here.*
MILAN	*And you do it for that?*
ANNA	*I don't know, Milan. It seemed right.*
MILAN	*You've never liked your father.*
ANNA	*That doesn't stop me wanting the best for him. Maybe he just makes me feel guilty for not suffering like him.*

SHE PUSHES PAST HIM AND INTO THE KITCHEN

ROBERT	(TO **MILAN** – INDIGNANTLY) I understood some of that.
JAMES	Oh for goodness sake, Robert. You are so bloody self-righteous. Anna fucked you because she wanted a free trip to America. No harm done. But just cool it. OK?
ROBERT	I don't understand you people.

JAMES   Obviously not.

ROBERT GOES OUT TO THE KITCHEN, WHERE ANNA HAS A BOWL OF WATER AND IS PUTTING DISINFECTANT IN IT. ROBERT FOLLOWS HER LIKE A DOG. THE DIALOGUE SPLITS – WITH JAMES, MILAN AND B. TALKING IN THE LOUNGE / ANNA AND ROBERT IN THE KITCHEN.

JAMES	(*To B.*) What happened?		
B.	I told you. I see you too much.		
JAMES	I paid him.		
		ROBERT	Is that true?
B.	Not enough. He said not enough.		
		ANNA	Is what true?
		ROBERT	That you only went to bed with me because you wanted to go to America?
		ANNA	Milan was waving a gun about—
		ROBERT	He didn't force you to say it.
		ANNA	I told him what he wanted to hear.
MILAN	Is the Madonna a present for him?		
JAMES	(*ignoring Milan. To B.*) Christ Almighty, I paid a bloody fortune.	ROBERT	Did you?
		ANNA	He let me have the gun, didn't he.
B. TAKES A SCRUMPLED NOTE FROM A POCKET AND GIVES IT TO JAMES. JAMES READS IT.			
		ROBERT	Is it true?
		ANNA	I took you to the Church / didn't I.
		ROBERT	Is it?
JAMES	He says it's a warning. You had rules.		
		ANNA	Did I ever once say I wanted you to take me to America?
MILAN	The Icon. It's your gift for him. Isn't it? It is. For him.		
JAMES	The Icon should be in a Gallery.	ROBERT	I have to ask, Anna.
		ANNA	Why? Don't you trust me? Don't you trust yourself?

JAMES We made a trade, Milan. I don't ask you what you want your Bible for.	**ROBERT** I'm only asking.
JAMES CRADLES **B.** IN HIS ARMS, AND WOULD OFFER HIM MORE WARMTH IF HE WERE NOT SO DISTRACTED BY **MILAN** – WHO IS INSCRUTABLE. HE SAYS NOTHING, DOES NOTHING. AND, BY DOING NOTHING, IS VERY THREATENING.	**ANNA** Why? Why do you need to ask? .... I took you to the Church. .... Alright, yes, Id like to go to America. I'd like to go to China. I'd like to go to Brazil. Going to America's not why I slept with you. You know damn well it's not why I slept with you.
A LONG WAIT BETWEEN **JAMES**'s LINE ABOUT THE BIBLE AND MILAN's NEXT LINE.	**ROBERT** Why, then? **ANNA** I desired you, Robert. Is that so hard to believe? James and I have a good relationship; but there's never been a lot of sex. I like sex, Robert. Is that why you want to punish me now?
	ROBERT I don't want to punish you. Of course I don't want to punish you. *silence*
silence **MILAN** He's your fucking queer boy.	
MILAN WAITS FOR **JAMES** TO REACT, BUT **JAMES** REFUSES TO BE DRAWN.	**ANNA** Milan is dangerous, Robert. I'd tell him I'd slept with the Pope if it meant we could all be sure of getting out of here safely. ....
MILAN SPITS ON **JAMES** AND **B.** **B.** IS TOO WEARY TO OFFER MUCH RESISTANCE, AND **JAMES** GESTURES QUIETLY TO STOP HIM RETALIATING. GIVEN MILAN'S HOSTILITY, IT IS QUITE BRAVE OF **JAMES** TO WIPE EACH OF THEIR FACES WITH A PRISTINE HANDKERCHIEF.	You still don't believe me, do you. What about the Synagogue? I took you to the Synagogue. How do you think that felt? **ROBERT** I don't know.... You don't talk about it. **ANNA** I told you as much as I have ever told anybody.
MILAN QUICKLY REVERTS TO HIS INSCRUTABLE EXPRESSION.	**ROBERT** But you don't talk about it.
JAMES TRIES NOT TO BE INTIMIDATED	**ANNA** Of course I don't talk about it. I tell you I feel guilty about my Dad. You think that's easy to tell someone? What the fuck more do you want from me, Robert?
JAMES At least you're away from them .... You're safe now... It'll be alright. I promise.	**ROBERT** I care about you.
	ANNA You ask so stupid questions, Robert. How about 'Why did WE sleep together, Robert?' I tell you something: I don't know. Because everybody makes fucking

		stupid mistakes sometimes, Robert. That's why. Is that what you want to hear? What don't you talk about, Robert? What about your parents, Robert? Tell me about them. What are they? Mormons? Amish? CIA? You _accuse_ me of sleeping with you. You don't know how to care about me.
BUT WHEN **JAMES** LOOKS AT **B.** HE REALISES THAT HE HAS NO IDEA WHAT TO DO NEXT. HE CALLS THROUGH TO THE KITCHEN:	**ROBERT**	Of course I care about you. I care about you more than —
	ANNA	Why shouldn't I want to go to America? You wanted to come to Hungary. It was you wanted to take me back to America. 'What'll I say to my kid brother?' Remember that? You're not interested in me. It's the experience you wanted. The Hungarian woman. Exotic isn't it.
JAMES Anna....		
	ROBERT	Jeez, Anna. There's no way.... I know you're upset. I just want to understand. Don't you see that?
silence		_silence_
JAMES Anna...	**ANNA**	I'd like to.
	ROBERT	Why do you feel so guilty about your Dad?
	ANNA	Because I hate him. Because I want to get him out of here. Because I like the new Hungary. Because he stinks. And I have to put him in the bath. And if I left him there he'd drown. And he's forgotten who I am.
JAMES Anna...		So he looks at me like I'm a nurse and oh fuck it Robert I don't want to talk about it.

B.   You have to get me out of Hungary

JAMES   I'm afraid / that England's

B.   You have to get / me to England.

JAMES   not too keen on refugees at the moment.   But we'll do something. I promise. You'll be alright.

ANNA COMES IN FROM THE KITCHEN WITH HER BOWL OF WATER AND DISINFECTANT, SOME CLOTH AND A TOWEL. SHE TAKES THE CLOTH, SOAKS IT IN THE WATER AND STARTS TRYING TO CLEAN UP **B**'s FACE. **B**. FLINCHES AS HE DOES SO. JAMES WATCHES, TAKING A STRANGE DELIGHT IN **ANNA'S** UNEXPECTED TENDERNESS.

B.   I cannot go back.

JAMES   We'll find you somewhere.

B.   How can I work? You said I could be in movies.

ANNA   He said what?

63

JAMES I'll get you into a hospital. A good surgeon / will be able to ...

ROBERT I'm sorry, Anna.

MILAN You, too?

ROBERT ?

MILAN (PUTTING ON HIS COD SERBIAN ACCENT AGAIN FOR ONE LAST TIME) I also
      am sorry. Yes?

silence ....

AND THEN IN A SUDDEN FLURRY OF VIOLENCE, **MILAN** GETS OUT A KNIFE AND
STABS **JAMES**.

First you take Anna from me, then you treat her like shit. You shit on her you shit on me.
You and your fucking queer boy.

MILAN IS ABOUT TO ATTACK **B**. WHEN **ROBERT** GRABS **MILAN** AND FLOORS HIM. FOR A WHILE IT SEEMS THAT **ROBERT** IS GETTING THE WORST OF IT – AND ONLY JUST MANAGING TO AVOID SERIOUS INJURY. IN THE STRUGGLE HE IS CUT BUT EVENTUALLY SUCCEEDS IN LOOSENING **MILAN'S** HOLD ON THE KNIFE – WHICH GOES SPINNING TO THE OTHER SIDE OF THE ROOM. HOWEVER, **MILAN** NOW HAS **ROBERT** IN A DEADLY HOLD – HIS FOREARM ACROSS **ROBERT'S** THROAT.	*AT THE SAME TIME AS MILAN AND ROBERT ARE FIGHTING ...* JAMES IS BLEEDING PROFUSELY; BUT ALTHOUGH SHOCKED AND WEAK HE IS CAPABLE OF MOVEMENT. JAMES GOES TO MILAN'S KIT-BAG. WITH DIFFICULTY, HE UNDOES THE CORD AT THE TOP AND REACHES IN.

ROBERT Anna, get him off me. Anna. Get him off me.

ANNA How can I? How can I? ... *Milan. Stop it. Stop it. Stop it.* (S-C)

SHE TRIES TO PULL HIM OFF. BUT THIS ONLY STRENGTHENS **MILAN'S** RESOLVE.
JAMES HAS GOT THE RIFLE OUT OF **MILAN'S** KIT BAG; AND HAS STARTED TO
ASSEMBLE IT. HE LETS THE KIT BAG FALL, SO THE TOP IS CLOSE TO **ROBERT'S** FREE
HAND.

MILAN *He wants to kill me, Anna. If I let go of him he'll kill me.* (H)

WITH A FLAILING HAND, **ROBERT** GRABS THE CORD TYING THE OPENING OF THE KIT-
BAG. HE PULLS IT OFF THE BAG. HE TRIES TO TALK, BUT CANNOT ARTICULATE
ANYTHING.

THEN HE MANAGES TO WRAP THE CORD ROUND **MILAN'S** THROAT AND STARTS TO
TIGHTEN IT. **MILAN** AND **ROBERT** BOTH CHOKING.

JAMES *Milan, let go of him.* (H)

AT THE SAME TIME BOTH **ANNA** AND **MILAN** LOOK UP AND SEE THE GUN. THE SHOCK
OF SEEING **JAMES** WITH THE GUN MAKES **MILAN** MOMENTARILY LOOSEN HIS GRIP
ON **ROBERT**. **ROBERT** PULLS THE CORD TIGHTER.

ANNA James. What are you doing?

MILAN   *Get him off me.*   (H)

ANNA   Let him go. Robert. Robert.

BUT **ROBERT** IS CONVINCED THAT IF HE LETS GO, **MILAN** WILL BE BACK AT HIM. HAVING GOT THE UPPER HAND HE IS NOT GOING TO LOSE IT.

ROBERT   He's mad. He's a fucking psycho. How can I let him go?

ANNA   You'll kill him.

ANNA PULLS AT **ROBERT** TRYING TO DRAG HIM OFF; BUT THE HARDER SHE STRUGGLES WITH HIM, THE TIGHTER **ROBERT** PULLS THE CORD.

ROBERT   I've got you now, you bastard.

ANNA KICKS AT **ROBERT**, TRYING TO GET HIM OFF; BUT HE STILL HANGS ON TO THE CORD EVER TIGHTER, ALMOST HYSTERICAL WITH INTENSITY.

ANNA   Do something. Somebody. Do something.

B. GETS TO HIS FEET AND GRABS **ROBERT**, TWISTING HIS FACE AWAY FROM **MILAN** AND FORCING HIM OFF. FINALLY **ROBERT** HAS TO LET GO OF THE CORD. **MILAN** LIES LIMP ON THE FLOOR, NOT MOVING.

JAMES   (*To Robert*, THREATENING HIM WITH THE GUN) Move away. Go on.

ROBERT DOES AS HE'S TOLD. **ANNA** GOES TO MILAN AND CRADLES HIS HEAD.

ROBERT   I saved you. Don't you see that. I saved you. Both of you.

(i.e. **JAMES** AND **B.**)

ANNA   Milan?

SHE LISTENS FOR HIS BREATHING.

Milan?

ROBERT   Don't you see that? Don't you see that? What the Hell was he doing with a gun like that? He was crazy. He was mad.

JAMES DROPS THE GUN AND COLLAPSES BACK INTO THE SOFA, NEXT TO **B.**

JAMES   (*Now very weak*) Yes. Probably mad. I got it for him. He got me the Icon - I got him the gun.

ROBERT   You're crazy too

JAMES   He had a plan.

B. NOW TAKES THE CLOTH AND DIPS IT IN WATER, SOOTHES **JAMES**'s HEAD, TRIES TO STOP HIM TALKING.

He said he had a way to stop the fucking mess in Yugoslavia.

ANNA   Milan?

SHE LISTENS CLOSER TO HIS BREATHING AND HEARTBEAT. SHE LOOKS UP AT **ROBERT** ACCUSINGLY.

65

ROBERT   Shit, I didn't do it.   I didn't do it.   What else could I do?

             (HE STARTS TO SOB)

             ANNA TAKES OUT THE HANDGUN THAT **MILAN** HAD HANDED OVER TO HER. SHE SAYS NOTHING, BUT CONTINUES TO STARE AT **ROBERT** AS SHE REMOVES THE SAFETY CATCH. SHE KISSES MILAN FULL ON THE MOUTH, AND THEN LOOKS UP AGAIN.

ANNA   You want me to talk.... You want me to tell you things.

             SHE SHOOTS **ROBERT**, WHO IS BLOWN BACKWARDS BY THE FORCE OF THE BULLET BEFORE COLLAPSING.

silence

             ... AND THEN, ALMOST IMPERCEPTIBLY THE SOUND OF HELICOPTERS — AT FIRST SO QUIET IT COULD ALMOST BE THE SOUND OF AN AMPLIFIED HEARTBEAT. GETTING GRADUALLY LOUDER AND LOUDER UNTIL – WHEN DIRECTLY OVERHEAD AND DEAFENING – THE SOUND OF THE THUMPING HELICOPTER BLADES METAMORPHOSES INTO THE SOUND OF GUNFIRE.

             THE SOUND SUDDENLY CUTS

Brian Woolland's previous writing for theatre includes *Getting Over You* (Etcetera Theatre 1995, revived in Szeged, Hungary, 1996), *Treason's Peace* (Soho Theatre, 1994, revived at The Dukes Playhouse, Lancaster, 2002) and a series of T.I.E. plays for Spiral Theatre Company: *Away Games*, *Perpetual Motion* and *Streetwise in Paradise*, all of which also explore issues of language and identity. *Away Games* toured extensively throughout England, France and Germany. *Double Tongue* was his first play for Border Crossings. Since the revival of *Getting Over You* in Szeged, he has been a frequent visitor to Hungary. He is also the co-author of *Ben Jonson and Theatre* (Routledge, 1999) and the editor of *Jonsonians: Living Traditions* (Ashgate, 2004). His book about the theatre of Peter Barnes is to be published by Methuen early in 2004. He is currently working on a new play for Border Crossings and a novel – a political thriller about Green terrorism.